Visual Thinking
For Information Design

The Morgan Kaufmann Series in Interactive Technologies

Series Editors:
- Stuart Card, PARC
- Jonathan Grudin, Microsoft
- Jakob Nielsen, Nielsen Norman Group

Evaluating Children's Interactive Products: Principles and Practices for Interaction Designers
Panos Markopoulus, Janet Read, Stuart MacFarlane and Johanna Hoysniemi

HCI Beyond the GUI; Design for Haptic, Speech, Olfactory and Other Non-Traditional Interfaces
Edited by Philip Kortum

Measuring the User Experience; Collecting, Analyzing, and Presenting Usability Metrics
Tom Tullis and Bill Albert

Keeping Found Things Found: The Study and Practice of Personal Information Management
William Jones

GUI Bloopers 2.0: Common User Interface Design Don'ts and Dos
Jeff Johnson

Visual Thinking: For Design
Colin Ware

Moderating Usability Tests: Principles and Practice for Interacting
Joseph Dumas and Beth Loring

User-Centered Design Stories: Real-World UCD Case Studies
Carol Righi and Janice James

Sketching User Experience: Getting the Design Right and the Right Design
Bill Buxton

Text Entry Systems: Mobility, Accessibility, Universality
Scott MacKenzie and Kumiko Tanaka-ishi

Letting Go of the Words: Writing Web Content that Works
Janice "Ginny" Redish

Personas and User Archetypes: A Field Guide for Interaction Designers
Jonathan Pruitt and Tamara Adlin

Cost-Justifying Usability
Edited by Randolph Bias and Deborah Mayhew

User Interface Design and Evaluation
Debbie Stone, Caroline Jarrett, Mark Woodroffe, Shailey Minocha

Rapid Contextual Design
Karen Holtzblatt, Jessamyn Burns Wendell, and Shelley Wood

Voice Interaction Design: Crafting the New Conversational Speech Systems
Randy Allen Harris

Understanding Users: A Practical Guide to User Requirements: Methods, Tools, and Techniques
Catherine Courage and Kathy Baxter

The Web Application Design Handbook: Best Practices for Web-Based Software
Susan Fowler and Victor Stanwick

The Mobile Connection: The Cell Phone's Impact on Society
Richard Ling

Information Visualization: Perception for Design, 2nd Edition
Colin Ware

Interaction Design for Complex Problem Solving: Developing Useful and Usable Software
Barbara Mirel

The Craft of Information Visualization: Readings and Reflections
Written and edited by Ben Bederson and Ben Shneiderman

HCI Models, Theories, and Frameworks: Towards a Multidisciplinary Science
Edited by John M. Carroll

Observing the User Experience: A Practitioner's Guide to User Research
Mike Kuniavsky

Paper Prototyping: The Fast and Easy Way to Design and Refine User Interfaces
Carolyn Snyder

Visual Thinking
For Information Design

Colin Ware

Second Edition

Amsterdam • Boston • Heidelberg • London • New York • Oxford
Paris • San Diego • San Francisco • Singapore • Sydney • Tokyo
Morgan Kaufmann is an imprint of Elsevier

Morgan Kaufmann is an imprint of Elsevier
50 Hampshire Street, 5th Floor, Cambridge, MA 02139, United States

British Library Cataloguing-in-Publication Data
A catalogue record for this book is available from the British Library.

Library of Congress Cataloging-in-Publication Data
A catalog record for this book is available from the Library of Congress.

ISBN: 978-0-12-823567-6

For Information on all Morgan Kaufmann publications
visit our website at https://www.elsevier.com/books-and-journals

Publisher: Katey Birtcher
Acquisitions Editor: Steve Merken
Editorial Project Manager: Alice Grant
Production Project Manager: Manikandan Chandrasekaran
Cover Designer: Brian Salisbury

Typeset by MPS Limited, Chennai, India

Printed in India

Last digit is the print number: 9   8   7   6   5   4   3   2   1

Contents

Preface

The motivation behind this second edition of *Visual Thinking* is a new theory of human memory and cognition known as *predictive cognition;* it is radically changing how we should understand visual thinking. In essence the theory holds that memories are not passive repositories of information about our past. Instead, they are predictive mental models that guide our future actions; their role in reminiscing is secondary. Predictive cognition theory is especially useful when we are designing visualizations to be part of presentations. The key is to think about the predictive mental models in the minds of audience members and how the right kinds of visualizations may enhance those mental models. This theory provides the framework for an all-new Chapter 8, which is about the design of presentation visuals.

This book also embraces the *active vision* theory of human perception, which predates predictive cognition and provides its foundation. Active vision means that we should think about graphic designs as cognitive tools, enhancing and extending our brains. Although we can, to some extent, form mental images in our heads, we do much better when those images are out in the world, on paper or on computer screen. Diagrams, maps, web pages, information graphics, visual instructions, and technical illustrations all help us to solve problems through a process of visual thinking. We are all cognitive cyborgs in this Internet age in the sense that we rely heavily on cognitive tools to amplify our mental abilities. Visual thinking tools are especially important because they harness the visual pattern-finding part of the brain. Almost half the brain is devoted to the visual sense, and the visual brain is exquisitely capable of interpreting graphical patterns, even scribbles, in many different ways. Often, to see a pattern is to understand the solution to a problem.

The active vision revolution is all about understanding perception as a dynamic process. Scientists used to think that we had rich images of the world in our heads built up from the information coming in through the eyes. Now we know that we only have the illusion of seeing the world in detail. In fact, the brain grabs just those fragments that are needed to execute the current mental activity. The brain directs the eyes to move, tunes up parts of itself to receive the expected input, and extracts exactly what is needed for our current thinking activity, whether that is reading a map, making a peanut butter and jelly sandwich, or looking at a poster. Our impression of a rich detailed world comes from the fact that we have the capability to extract anything we want at any moment through a movement of the eye that is literally faster than thought. This is automatic and so quick that we are unaware of doing it, giving us the illusion that we see stable detailed reality everywhere. The process of visual thinking is a kind of dance with the environment with some information stored internally and some externally, and it is by understanding this dance that we can understand how graphic designs can help us think.

Active vision has profound implications for design, and this is the subject of this book.

It is a book about how we think visually and what that understanding can tell us about how to design visual images. Understanding active vision tells us which colors and shapes will stand out clearly, how to organize space, and when we should use images instead of words to convey an idea.

Early on in the writing and image creation process I decided to "eat my own dog food" and apply active vision-based principles to the design of this book. One of these principles being that when text and images are related, they should be placed in close proximity. This is not as easy as it sounds. It turns out that there is a reason why there are labeled figure legends in academic publishing (e.g., Figure 1, Figure 2, etc.). It makes the job of the compositor much easier. A compositor is a person whose specialty is to pack images and words on the page *without reading the text*. This leads to the labeled figure and the parenthetical phrase often found in academic publishing, "see Figure X". This formula means that Figure X need not be on the same page as the accompanying text. It is a bad idea from the design perspective and a good idea from the perspective of the publisher. I decided to integrate text and words and avoid the use of "see Figure X," and the result was a difficult process and some conflict with a modern publishing house that does not, for example, invite authors to design meetings, even when the book is about design. The result is something of a design compromise, but I am grateful to the individuals at Elsevier who helped me with what has been a challenging exercise.

There are many people who have helped. Diane Cerra with Elsevier was patient with the difficult demands I made and full of helpful advice when I needed it. Denise Penrose guided me through the later stages and came up with the compromise solution that is realized in these pages. Dennis Shaeffer and Alisa Andreola helped with the design, and Mary James with the production process. My wife, Dianne Ramey, read the whole thing twice and fixed a very great number of grammar and punctuation errors. I am very grateful to Paul Catanese of the New Media Department at San Francisco State University and David Laidlaw of the Computer Graphics Group at Brown University who provided content reviews and told me what was clear and what was not. I did major revisions to Chapters 3 and 9 as a result of their input. For the second edition, Alice Grant and Manikandan Chandrasekaran helped with the production process.

This book is an introduction to what the burgeoning science of perception can tell us about visual design. It is intended for anyone who does design in a visual medium, and it should be of special interest to anyone who does graphic design for the Internet or who designs information graphics of one sort or another. Design can take ideas from anywhere, from art and culture as well as particular design genres. Science can enrich the mix.

Colin Ware
December 2020

Chapter 1

Visual Queries

When we are awake, with our eyes open, we have the impression that we see the world vividly, completely, and in detail. But this impression is dead wrong. As scientists have devised increasingly elaborate tests to find out what is stored in the brain about the state of the visual world at any instant, the same answer has come back again and again—at any given instant, we apprehend only a tiny amount of the information in our surroundings, but it is usually just the right information to carry us through the task of the moment.

We cannot even remember new faces unless we are specifically paying attention. Consider the following remarkable "real-world" experiment carried out by psychologists Daniel Simons and Daniel Levin.* A trained actor approached an unsuspecting member of the public, map in hand and in a crowded place with lots of pedestrian traffic, and began to ask for directions. Then, by means of a clever maneuver involving two workmen and a door, a second actor replaced the first in the middle of the conversation.

*D.J. Simons and D.T. Levin, 1998. Failure to detect changes to people during a real world interaction. *Psychonomic Bulletin and Review.* 5: 644–669.

Actor with map asks unsuspecting member of the public for directions.

Eager to help.

Workmen (also actors) arrive with door. The two must step apart to get out of the way.

Original actor with map creeps away.

A second actor resumes the request for information.

Unsuspecting member of the public fails to notice they are talking to a different person!

The second actor could have different clothing and different hair color, yet more than 50 percent of the time the unsuspecting participants failed to notice the substitution. Incredibly, people even failed to notice a change in gender! In some of the experiments, a male actor started the dialogue and a female actor was substituted under the cover of the two workmen with the door, but still most people failed to spot the switch.

What is going on here? On the one hand we have a subjective impression of being aware of everything, on the other hand, it seems, we see very little. How can this extraordinary finding be reconciled with our vivid impression that we see the whole visual environment? The solution, as psychologist Kevin O'Regan♦ puts it, is that "[t]he world is its own memory." We see very little at any given instant, but we can sample any part of our visual environment so rapidly with swift eye movement that we think we have all of it at once in our consciousness experience. We get what we need when we need it. The reason why the unwitting participants in Simons and Levin's experiment failed to notice the changeover was that they were doing their best to concentrate on the map, and although they had undoubtedly glanced at the face of the person holding it, that information was not critical and was not retained. We have very little attentional capacity, and information unrelated to our current task is quickly replaced with something we need right now.

There is a very general lesson here about seeing and cognition. The brain, like all biological systems, has become optimized over millennia of evolution. Brains have a very high level of energy consumption and must be kept as small as possible, or our heads would topple us over. Keeping a copy of the world in our brains would be a huge waste of cognitive resources and completely unnecessary. It is much more efficient to have rapid access to the actual world—to see only what we attend to and only attend to what we need—for the task at hand.

♦Kevin O'Regan's essay on the nature of the consciousness illusion brings into clear focus the fact that there is a major problem to be solved: how do we get a subjective impression of perceiving a detailed world, while all available evidence shows that we pick up very little information? It also points to the solution—just-in-time processing. J.K. O'Regan, 1992. Solving the "real" mysteries of visual perception: The world as an outside memory. *Canadian Journal of Psychology*. 46: 461–488.

The one-tenth of a second or so that it takes to make an eye movement is such a short time in terms of the brain's neuron-based processing clock that it seems instantaneous. Our illusory impression that we are constantly aware of everything happens because our brains arrange for eye movements to occur and the particularly relevant information to be picked up just as we turn our attention to something we need. We do not have the whole visual world in conscious awareness. In truth, we have very little, but we can get anything we need through mechanisms that are rapid and unconscious. We are unaware that time has passed and cognitive effort has been expended. Exactly how we get the task-relevant information and construct meaning from it is a central focus of this book.

The understanding that we only sample the visual world on a kind of need-to-know basis leads to a profoundly different model of perception, one that has only emerged over the last decade or so. This new understanding is central to the account of visual thinking set forth in this book.

According to this new view, visual thinking is a process that has the allocation of attention as its very essence. Attention, however, is multifaceted. Making an eye movement is an act of attending. The image on the retina is analyzed by further attention-related processes that tune our pattern-finding mechanisms to pull out the pattern most likely to help with whatever we are doing. At a cognitive level, we allocate scarce "working memory" resources to briefly retain in focal attention only to those pieces of information most likely to be useful. Seeing is all about attention. This new understanding leads to a revision of our thinking about the nature of visual consciousness. It is more accurate to say that we are conscious of the *field of information* to which we have *rapid access* rather than that we are immediately conscious of the world.

This new understanding also allows us to think about graphic design issues from a new and powerful perspective. We can now begin to develop a science of graphic design based on a scientific understanding of visual attention and pattern perception. To the extent to which it is possible to set out the message of this book in a single statement, the message is this: *Visual thinking consists of a series of acts of attention, driving eye movements, and tuning our pattern-finding circuits*. These acts of attention are called *visual queries*, and understanding how visual queries work can make us better designers. When we interact with an information display, such as a map, diagram, chart, graph, or a poster on the wall, we are usually trying to solve some kind of cognitive problem. In the case of the map, it may be how to get from one location to another. In the case of the graph, it may be to determine the trend; for example, is the population increasing or decreasing over time? What is the shape of the trend? The answers to our questions can be obtained by a series of searches for particular patterns—visual queries.

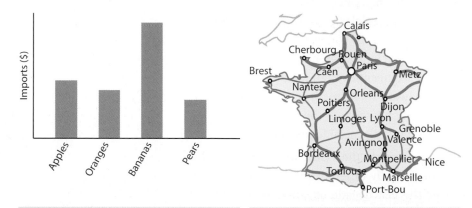

To find out which kind of fruit import is the largest by dollar value, we make visual queries to find the tallest bar, then find and read the label beneath.

To find a fast route, we first make visual queries to find the starting and ending cities, then we make queries to find a connected red line, indicative of fast roads, between those points.

At this point, you may be considering an obvious objection. What about the occasions when we are not intensely involved in some particular task? Surely we are not continually constructing visual queries when we are sitting in conversation with someone, or strolling along a sidewalk, or listening to music. There are two answers to this. The first is that, indeed, we are not always thinking visually with reference to the external environment; for example, we might be musing about the verbal content of a conversation we had over the telephone. The second is we are mostly unaware of just how structured and directed our seeing processes are. Even when we are in face-to-face conversation with someone, we constantly monitor facial expressions, the gestures, and gaze direction of that person, to pick up cues that supplement verbal information. If we walk on a path along the sidewalk of a city, we constantly monitor for obstacles and choose a path to take into account the other pedestrians. Our eyes make anticipatory movements to bumps and stones that may trip us, and our brains detect anything that may be on a trajectory to cross our path, triggering an eye movement to monitor it. Seeing while walking is, except on the smoothest and most empty road, a highly structured process.

To flesh out this model of visual thinking, we need to introduce key elements of the apparatus of vision and how each element functions.

THE APPARATUS AND PROCESS OF SEEING

The eyes are something like little digital cameras. They contain lenses that focus an image on the eyeball. Many find the fact that the image is upside-down at the back of the eye to be a problem. But the brain is a computer, albeit quite unlike a digital silicon-based one, and it is as easy for the brain to compute with an upside-down image as a right-side-up image.

Just as a digital camera has an array of light-sensitive elements recording three different color values, so the eye also has an array of light-sensitive cones recording three different colors (leaving aside rods♦). The analogy goes still further. Just as digital cameras compress image data for more compact transmission and storage, so several layers of cells in the retina extract what is most useful. As a result, information can be transmitted from the 100 million receptors in the eye to the brain by means of only 1 million fibers in the optic nerve.

There is, however, a profound difference between the signal sent from the eye to the back of the brain for early-stage processing and the signal sent to a memory chip from the pixel array of a digital camera. *Brain pixels* are concentrated in a central region called the *fovea*, whereas camera pixels are arranged in a uniform grid. Also, brain pixels function as little image-processing computers, not just passive recorders.

Visual detail can only be seen via the fovea, at the very center of the visual field. Our vision is so good in this region that each eye can resolve

♦The human eye actually contains four different receptor types, three cone types and rods. However, because rods function mainly only at low light levels, in our modern, brightly lit world we can for all practical purposes treat the eye as a three-receptor system. It is because of this that we need only three different wavelength receptors in digital cameras.

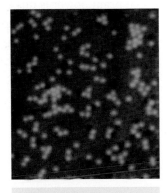

At the back of the eye is a mosaic of photoreceptors. Each responds to the amount of light falling on it. This example shows the central foveal region where three different cone receptors register different colors of light.

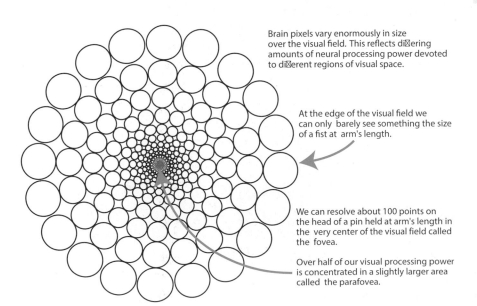

Brain pixels vary enormously in size over the visual field. This reflects differing amounts of neural processing power devoted to different regions of visual space.

At the edge of the visual field we can only barely see something the size of a fist at arm's length.

We can resolve about 100 points on the head of a pin held at arm's length in the very center of the visual field called the fovea.

Over half of our visual processing power is concentrated in a slightly larger area called the parafovea.

about 100 points on the head of a pin held at arm's length, but the region is only about the size of our thumbnail held at arm's length. At the edge of the visual field, vision is terrible; we can just resolve something the size of a human head. For example, we may be vaguely aware that someone is standing next to us, but unless we have already glanced in that direction we will not know who it is.

The non-uniformity of the visual processing power is such that half our visual brain power is directed to processing less than 5 percent of the visual world. This is why we have to move our eyes; it is the only way we can get all that brain power directed where it will be most useful. Non-uniformity is also one of the key pieces of evidence showing that we do not comprehend the world all at once. We cannot possibly grasp it all at once since our nervous systems only process details in a tiny location at any one instant.

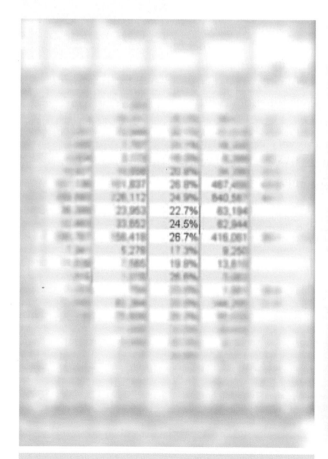

We only process details in the center of the visual field. We pick up information by directing our foveae using rapid eye movements.

At the edge of the visual field, we can barely see that someone is standing next to us.

The term brain pixel was introduced earlier by way of contrast with digital camera pixels. Brain pixels provide a kind of distorted neural map covering the whole visual field. There are a great many tiny ones processing information from central regions where we direct our gaze and only a few very large ones processing information at the edge of the visual field. Because of this, we cannot see much out of the corners of our eyes.

Strong eye muscles attached to each eyeball rotate it rapidly so that different parts of the visual world become imaged on the central high-resolution fovea. The muscles accelerate the eyeball to an angular velocity of up to 900 degrees per second, then stop it, all in less than one-tenth of a second. This movement is called a saccade, and during a saccadic eye movement vision is suppressed. The eyes move in a series of jerks pointing the fovea at interesting and useful locations, pausing briefly at each, before flicking to the next point of interest. Controlling these eye movements is a key part of the skill of seeing.

We do not see the world as jerky, nor for the most part are we aware of moving our eyes, and this adds yet more evidence that we do not perceive what is directly available through our visual sense.

This illustration is based on a slice through the head of the visible man at the level of the eyeballs. Its color has been altered to show the eye muscles and the eyeballs more clearly.

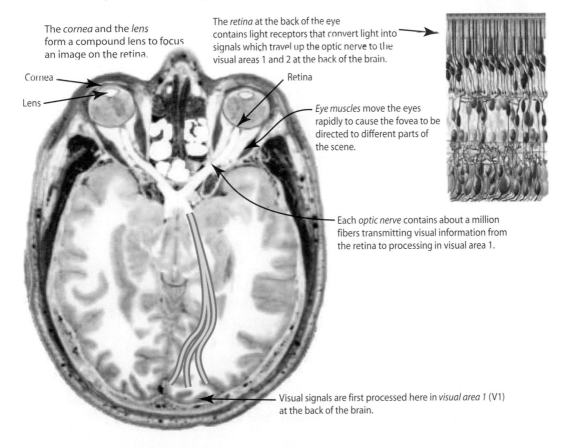

The *cornea* and the *lens* form a compound lens to focus an image on the retina.

Cornea

Lens

The *retina* at the back of the eye contains light receptors that convert light into signals which travel up the optic nerve to the visual areas 1 and 2 at the back of the brain.

Retina

Eye muscles move the eyes rapidly to cause the fovea to be directed to different parts of the scene.

Each *optic nerve* contains about a million fibers transmitting visual information from the retina to processing in visual area 1.

Visual signals are first processed here in *visual area 1* (V1) at the back of the brain.

THE ACT OF PERCEPTION

The visual field has a big hole in it. Cover your left eye and look at the X. Move the page nearer and further away, being sure to keep the X and the B horizontally aligned.

At some point the B should disappear. This is because the image of the B is falling on the blind spot, a region of the retina where the optic nerve and blood vessels enter the eye and there are no receptors. We are unaware that we have this hole in our visual field. The brain does not know that it has a blind spot, just as it does not know how little of the world we see at each moment. This is more evidence that seeing is not at all a passive registration of information. Instead it is active and constructive.

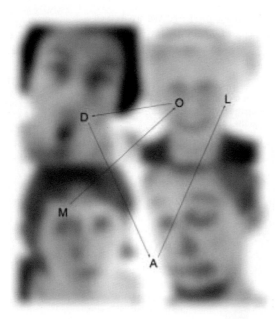

Broadly speaking, the act of perception is determined by two kinds of processes: *bottom-up*, driven by the visual information in the pattern of light falling on the retina, and *top-down*, driven by the demands of attention, which in turn are determined by the needs of the tasks. The picture shown above is designed to demonstrate how top-down attention can influence what you see and how.

First look at the letters and lines. Start with the M and follow the sequence of lines and letters to see what word is spelled. You will find yourself making a series of eye movements focusing your visual attention on the small area of each letter in turn. You will, of course, notice the faces in the background but as you perform the task they will recede from your consciousness.

Next look at the faces and try to interpret their expressions. You will find yourself focusing in turn on each of the faces and its specific features, such as the mouth or eyes, but also as you do this the letters and lines will recede from your consciousness. Thus, what you see depends on both the information in the pattern on the page as it is processed bottom-up through the various neural processing stages, and on the top-down effects of attention that determines both where you look and what you pull out from the patterns on the page.

There are actually two waves of neural activity that occur when our eye alights on a point of interest. An information-driven wave passes information first to the back of the brain along the optic nerve, then sweeps forward to the forebrain, and an attention-driven wave originates in the attention control centers of the forebrain and sweeps back, enhancing the most relevant information and suppressing less relevant information.

The neural machinery of the visual system is modular in the sense that distinct regions of the brain perform specific kinds of computation before passing the processed information on to some other region. The visual system has at least two dozen distinct processing modules, each performing some different computational task, but for the purposes of this

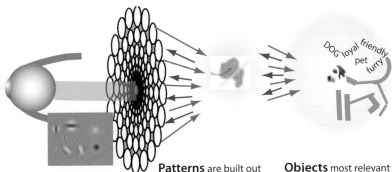

Features are processed in parallel from every part of the visual field. Millions of features are processed simultaneously.

Patterns are built out of features depending on attentional demands. Attentional tuning reinforces those most relevant.

Objects most relevant to the task at hand are held in Visual Working Memory. Only between one and three are held at any instant. Objects have both nonvisual and visual attributes.

Bottom-up information drives pattern building.

Top-down attentional processes reinforce relevant information.

overview we will simplify to a three-stage model. The processing modules are organized in a hierarchy, with information being transferred both up and down from low-level *feature* processors to *pattern* and *object* processors. We shall consider it first from a bottom-up perspective, and then from a top-down perspective.

BOTTOM-UP

In the bottom-up view, information is successively selected and filtered so that meaningless low-level features in the first stage form into patterns in the second stage, and meaningful objects in the third stage.

The main *feature-processing* stage occurs after information arrives in the V1 cortex having traveled up the optic nerve. There are more neurons devoted to this stage than any other. Perhaps as many as five billion neurons form a massively parallel processing machine simultaneously operating on information from only one million fibers in the optic nerve. Feature detection is done by several different kinds of brain pixel processors that are arranged in a distorted map of visual space. Some pull out little bits of size and orientation information, so that every part of the visual field is simultaneously processed for the existence of oriented edges or contours. Others compute red-green differences and yellow-blue differences, and still others process the elements of motion and the elements of stereoscopic depth. The brain has sufficient neurons in this stage to process every part of the visual field simultaneously for each kind of feature information. In later chapters, we will discuss how understanding feature processing can help us design symbols that stand out distinctly.

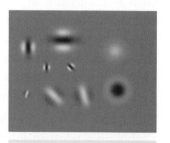

Some neurons that process elementary features respond to little packets of orientation and size information. Others respond best to redness, yellowness, greenness, and blueness. Still others respond to different directions of motion.

At the intermediate level of the visual processing hierarchy, feature information is used to construct increasingly complex *patterns*. Visual space is divided up into regions of common texture and color. Long chains of features become connected to form continuous contours. Understanding how this occurs is critical for design because this is the level at which space becomes organized and different elements become linked or segregated. Some of the design principles that emerge at this level have been understood for over 70 years through the work of Gestalt psychology (*gestalt* means pattern in German). But there is also much that we have learned in the intervening years through the advent of modern neuroscience that refines and deepens our understanding.

At the top level of the hierarchy, information that has been processed from millions upon millions of simple features has been reduced and distilled through the pattern-processing stage to a small number of visual *objects*. The system that holds about three objects in attention at one time is called *visual*

At the intermediate pattern-finding stage of the visual system, patterns are formed out of elementary features. A string of features may form the boundary of a region having a particular color. The result is that the visual field is segmented into patterns.

working memory. The small capacity of visual working memory is the reason why, in the experiment described at the start of this chapter, people failed to recognize that they were speaking to a different person. The information about the person they were talking to became displaced from their visual (and verbal) working memories by more immediate task-relevant data.

Although something labeled "dog" might be one of the objects we hold in our visual working memory, there is nothing like a picture of a dog in the head; rather we have a few visual details of the dog that have been recently fixated. These visual details are linked to various kinds of information that we already know about dogs through a network of association, and therein lays the power of the system. Concepts that dogs are loyal, pets, furry, and friendly may become activated and ready for use. In addition, various possibilities for action may become activated leading to a heightened state of readiness. Actions such as petting the dog or avoiding the dog (depending on our concepts) become primed for activation. Of course if it is our own dog, "Millie," a much richer set of associations become activated and the possibilities for action more varied; our brain is predicting what the dog will do and preparing for responses. This momentary binding together of visual information with nonvisual concepts and action priming is central to what it means to perceive something.

The reason why we can make do with only three or four objects extracted from the blooming buzzing confusion of the world is that these few objects are made up of exactly what we need to help us perform the task of the moment. Each is a temporary nexus of meaning and action. Sometimes nexus objects are held in mind for a second or two; sometimes they only last for a tenth of a second. The greatly limited capacity of visual working memory is a major bottleneck in cognition, and it is the reason why we must often rely on external visual aids in the process of visual thinking.

It is tempting to think of visual working memory as the place real visual thinking occurs, but this is a mistake. One reason it is easy to think this way is that this is the way computers work. In a digital computer, all complex operations on data occur in the central processing unit. Everything else is about loading data, getting it lined up so that it is ready to be processed just when it is needed, and sending it back out again. The brain is not like this. There is actually far more processing going on in the lower-level feature-processing and pattern-finding systems of the brain than in the visual working memory. It is much more accurate to think of visual thinking as a multicomponent cognitive system. Each part does something that is relatively simple. For example, the intermediate pattern processors detect and pass on information about a particular red patch

When we see something, such as a dog, we do not simply form an image of that dog in our heads. Instead, the few features that we have directly fixated are bound together with the knowledge we have about dogs in general and this particular dog. Possible behaviors of the dog and actions we might take in response to it are also activated.

of color that happens to be imaged on a particular part of the retina. An instant later, this red patch may come to be labeled as "poppies."

In many ways, the real power of *visual* thinking rests in pattern finding. Often to see a pattern is to find a solution to a problem. Seeing the path to the door tells us how to get out of the room, and that path is essentially a kind of visual pattern. Similarly, seeing the relative sizes of segments in a pie chart tells us which company has the greatest market shares.

Responses to visual patterns can be thought of as another type of pattern. (To make this point we briefly extend the use of the word "pattern" beyond its restricted sense as something done at a middle stage in visual processing.) For most mundane tasks we do not think through our actions from first principles. Instead, a response pattern like walking toward the door is triggered from a desire to leave the room. Indeed it is possible to think of intelligence in general as a collaboration of pattern-finding processors.♦ A way of responding to a pattern is also a pattern, and usually one we have executed many times before. A very common pattern of seeing and responding is the movement of a mouse cursor to the corner of a computer interface window, together with a mouse click to close that window. Response patterns are the essence of the skills that bind perception to action. But they have their negative side too. They also cause us to ignore the great majority of the information that is available in the world so that we often miss things that are important.

♦This view of intelligence as a kind of hierarchy of pattern-finding systems has been elaborated in *On Intelligence* by Jeff Hawkins and Sandra Blakeslee (Times Books, New York. 2004).

TOP-DOWN

So far we have been focusing on vision as a bottom-up process:

$$\text{retinal image} \rightarrow \text{features} \rightarrow \text{patterns} \rightarrow \text{objects}$$

But every stage in this sequence contains corresponding top-down processes. In fact, there are more neurons sending signals back down the hierarchy than sending signals up the hierarchy.

We use the word *attention* to describe top-down processes. Top-down processes are driven by the need to accomplish some goal within the context of an ongoing loosely constructed model of the world and our place in it. This might be an action, such as reaching out and grasping a teacup, or exiting a room. It might be a cognitive goal, such as understanding an idea expressed in a diagram in order to update and improve part of the set of mental models whereby we understand and act. There is a constant linking and re-linking of visual information with different kinds of nonvisual information. There is also a constant *priming* of executable mental models so that if we have to act, we are ready. This linking and re-linking is the essence of high-level attention, but it also has implications for other lower-level processes.

At the low level of feature and elementary pattern analysis, top-down attention causes a bias in favor of the signals we are looking for. If we are looking for red spots then the red spot detectors will signal louder. If we are looking for slanted lines then slanted line feature detectors will have their signal enhanced. This biasing in favor of what we are seeking or anticipating occurs at every stage of processing. What we end up actually perceiving is the result of information about the world strongly biased according to what we are attempting to accomplish.

Perhaps the most important attentional process is the sequencing of eye movements. Psychologist Mary Hayhoe and computer scientist Dana Ballard collaborated in using a new technology that tracked individuals' eye movements while they were able to move freely.[*] This allowed them to study natural eye movements "in the wild" instead of the traditional laboratory setup with their heads rigidly fixed in a special apparatus.

[*]M. Hayhoe and D. Ballard, 2005. Eye movements in natural behavior. *Trends in Cognitive Science.* 9(4): 188–194.

The sequence of eye movements made by someone making a peanut butter and jelly sandwich. The yellow circles show the eye fixations.

They had people carry out everyday tasks, such as making a peanut butter and jelly sandwich, and discovered a variety of eye movement patterns. Typically, people used bursts of rapid eye movements when they first encountered the tools and ingredients laid out in front of them. This presumably allowed them to get a feel for the overall layout of the workspace. Each of these initial fixations was brief, usually one-tenth of a second or less. Once people got to work, they would make much longer fixations so that they could, for example, spread the peanut butter on the bread. Generally, there was great economy in that objects were rarely looked at unnecessarily; instead, they were fixated using a "just-in-time strategy." When people were performing some action, such as placing a lid on a jar, they did not look at what their hands were doing but looked ahead to the jar lid while one hand moved to grasp it. Once the lid was in hand, they looked ahead to fixate the top of the jar enabling the next movement of the lid. There were occasional longer-term look-aheads, where people would glance at something they might need to use sometime in the next minute or two. The overall impression we get from this research is of a remarkably efficient, skilled visual process with perception and action closely linked—the dominant principle being that we only get the information we need, when we need it.

How do we decide where to move our eyes in a visual search task? If our brains have not processed the scene, how do we know where to look? But if we already know what is there, why do we need to look? It is a classic chicken and egg problem. The system seems to work roughly as follows.[*] Part of our brain constructs a crude map of the characteristics of the information that we need in terms of low-level features. Suppose I enter a supermarket produce section looking for oranges. My brain will tune my low-level feature receptors so that orange things send a stronger signal than patches of other colors. From this, a rough map of potential areas where there may be oranges will be constructed. Another part of my brain will construct a series of eye movements to all the potential areas on this spatial map. The eye movement sequence will be executed with a pattern processor checking off those areas where the target happened to be mangoes, or something else, so that they are not visited again. This process goes on until either oranges are found, or we decide they are probably hidden from view. This process, although efficient, is not always successful. For one thing, we have little color vision at the edges of the visual field, so it is necessary to land an eye movement near to oranges for the orange color–tuning process to work. When we are looking for bananas a shape-tuning process may also come into play so that regions with the distinctive curves of banana bunches can be used to aid the visual search.[•]

[*] J.R. Duhamel, C.L. Colby, and M.E. Goldberg. 1992. The updating of the representation of visual space in parietal cortex by intended eye movements. *Science*. Jan 3; 255(5040): 90–92.

[•] The book *Active Vision* by John Findlay and Ian Gilchrist (Oxford University Press, 2003) is an excellent introduction to the way eye movements are sequenced to achieve perception for action.

IMPLICATIONS FOR DESIGN

If we understand the world through just-in-time visual queries, the goal of information design must be to design displays so that *visual queries are processed both rapidly and correctly for every important cognitive task the display is intended to support*. This has a number of important ramifications for graphic design. The first is that in order to do successful design we must understand the cognitive tasks and visual queries a graphic is intended to support. This is normally done somewhat intuitively, but it can also be made explicit.

A map is perhaps the best example illustrating how graphic design can support a specific set of visual queries. Suppose we are lodged in a hotel near Ealing in West London, and we wish to go to a pub near Clapham Common where we will meet a friend. We would do well to consider the underground train system, and this will result is our formulating a number of cognitive tasks. We might like to know the following:

- Which combination of lines will get us to the pub?
- If there is more than one potential route, which is the shortest?
- What are the names of stations where train changes are needed?
- How long will the trip take?
- What is the distance between the hotel and its nearest underground station?
- What is the distance between the pub and its nearest underground station?
- How much will it cost?

Many of these tasks can be carried out through visual thinking with a map.

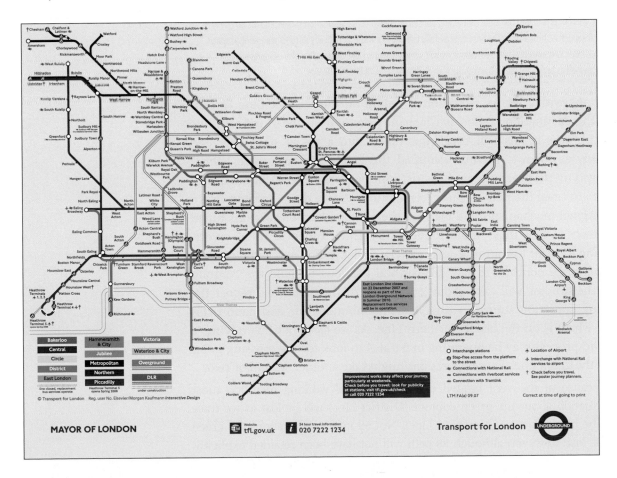

The famous London Underground map designed by Harry Beck is an excellent visual tool for carrying out some, but not all, of these tasks. Its clear schematic layout makes the reading of station names easy. The color coding of lines and the use of circles showing connection points make it relatively easy to visually determine routes that minimize the number of stops. The version shown on the previous page also provides rapidly accessible information about the fare structure through the gray and white zone bars.

Since we have previously used maps for route planning, we already have a cognitive plan for solving this kind of problem. It will likely consist of a set of steps something like the following.

STEP ONE is to construct a visual query to locate the station nearest to our hotel. Assuming we have the name of a station, this may take quite a protracted visual search since there are more than two hundred stations on the map; if, as is likely, we already have a rough idea where in London our hotel is located, this will narrow the search space.

STEP TWO is to visually locate a station near the pub, and this particular task is also not well supported. The famous map does support the station-finding task by spacing the labels for clear reading, but unlike other maps it does not give an index or a spatial reference grid.

STEP THREE is to find the route connecting our start station and our destination station. This visual query is very well supported by the map. The lines are carefully laid out in a way that radically distorts geographical space, but this is done to maintain clarity so that the visual tracing of lines is easy. Color coding also supports visual tracing, as well as providing labels that can be matched to the table of lines at the side.

Suppose that the start station is Ealing on the District Line (green) and the destination station is Clapham Common on the Northern Line (black). Our brains will break this down into a set of steps executed roughly as follows. Having identified the Ealing station and registered that it is on the green-colored District Line, we make a series of eye movements to trace the path of this green contour. As we do so, our top-down attentional mechanisms will increase the amplification on neurons tuned to green so that they "shout louder" than those tuned to other colors, making it easier for our mid-level pattern finder to find and connect parts of the green contour. It may take several fixations to build the contour, and the process will take about 2 seconds. At this point, we repeat the tracing operation starting with Clapham Common, our destination station, which is on the black Northern Line. As we carry out this tracing, a second process may be operating in parallel to look for the crossing point with the green line. These operations might take another second or two.

Because of the very limited capacity of visual working memory, most information about the green contour (District Line) will be lost as we trace out the black contour (Northern Line). Not all information about the green line is lost, however; although its path will not have been retained explicitly, considerable savings occur when we repeat an operation such as this. Repeating a tracing operation will take less cognitive effort, and require fewer fixations, than finding it in the first place. A hallmark of visual thinking is that it is often easier to redo some cognitive operation than to remember it.

Of course, the process may not be quite as straightforward as described. Much can go wrong. We may be visually sidetracked by the wrong branch of the Northern Line. The process is flexible and adaptive, and good visual thinkers have error-checking procedures. A final scan of the entire route will confirm that it is, indeed, a valid solution.

STEP FOUR is a visual query to get a rough estimate of how many stations there are on the route. This is unlikely to involve actual counting; instead, it will be a judgment that will be used together with prior experience to produce an estimate of the journey duration. This will naturally lead to misjudgments because the lengths of lines on the map do not correspond to travel times.

Our analysis shows that the London Underground map supports the visual route-finding step well but almost completely fails to support other planning steps such as finding a tube station near to the pub and estimating journey time. This is not to say that it is a bad design; the map is justifiably famous. The designers sacrificed spatial accuracy in favor of clear labels and routes, and therefore the map is very poor for providing information about the distance covered on the ground.

Having a computer behind an *interactive* graphic display takes the capability of visual cognitive tools to another level. Google Maps adds many cognitive supports that the underground map lacks: a map view that shows the underground lines in their spatial context, and a journey planner that provides information about how to get from a specific address to another specific address using London's buses and trains, complete with departure times and walking directions between transportation nodes.

Google Maps and other computer programs with visual interfaces add an additional dimension to the cognitive process. They allow for some parts of the computation process to occur in the brain, and other parts to occur in the computer program. Human and computer together form a *problem-solving system* with the screen display and the keyboard providing the interface. In later chapters, we further explore this rather mind-bending idea. For now, we return to the simpler case of visual thinking with a static graphic display.

NESTED LOOPS

A useful way of describing the way the brain operates to solve problems is as a set of nested loops. Outer loops deal with generalities. Inner loops process the details. In the outer loop, the brain constructs a set of steps to solve the problem and then executes them: find a map, find end point stations, trace lines, find intersections. This sequencing of the problem components is not in and of itself visual in nature; it is more likely to occur through the operations of verbal language subsystems of the brain. However, some problem components may be identified as having visual-thinking solutions, and these are used to construct visual queries on the display.

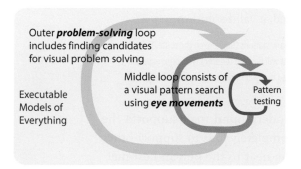

Outer **problem-solving** loop includes finding candidates for visual problem solving

Middle loop consists of a visual pattern search using **eye movements**

Pattern testing

Executable Models of Everything

The middle loop on the diagram is a visual search executed to find patterns that address the visual query. This involves executing a sequence of eye movements. In the previous example, this involved a visual tracing of the colored contours that represent train lines.

The inner loop is activated when the eye arrives at a point of fixation. A process of visual testing begins, and patterns within the central region of the visual field are evaluated at a rate of about 20 per second; although since the eye only stays in one place for less than two-tenths of a second, roughly one to four simple patterns may be evaluated on each fixation. In the example of finding the green line, this evaluation might have the following form. Is this contour green? Is it a continuation of the section of contour that was just registered?

The entire system operates within a system of what are called *executable predictive mental models* in modern neuroscience. Every part of the system is learning and adapting, and is designed for reuse.

Of course we are being metaphoric here. Nothing in the brain is making up questions and answering them. Rather, a neural process produces a signal that results in a change in the status of objects held in visual working memory. One such change in status would be that a neural representation of a green contour object becomes "bound" to another section of green contour in the temporary nexus and held together through the process called visual working memory.

Nested processes are characteristic of computer programs, but the ones executed by the brain are far more flexible and adaptive than those executed in a computer. They rely on patterns of action that have been built up over experience. We already have encoded in our memories visual search patterns for a huge number of situations, such as what we need to look for when entering a restaurant, looking at a web page, and driving a car toward an intersection. These are not, however, rigid rules, but rather like flexible plans that can be adapted to particular circumstances.

DISTRIBUTED COGNITION

This chapter has alluded to the existence of various brain structures and processes. In later chapters, specific areas of the brain where processes occur will be discussed in more detail. We will encounter visual areas, V1 and V2, specialized for parallel feature processing; V4, specialized for pattern processing; the fusiform gyrus, specialized for object processing; and the frontal lobes as well as midbrain areas, specialized for controlling high-level attention. The control of eye movements is mediated by mechanisms in the lateral interparietal area and superior colliculus. There are several dozen areas of the brain that have been mapped in animals using recordings from single neurons. Recent advances in brain scanning have allowed researchers to see which areas of the brain are most active when people perform specific visual tasks. The latest techniques even reveal the sequence in which different areas become active.

This is not, however, a book about neurophysiology, but a book about visual thinking. Its purpose is to provide a theoretical understanding of how we perceive in order to inform the design process. The names are useful but ultimately it does not matter exactly where in the brain something happens, instead it is important to know what kinds of visual information the brain can process efficiently. The timing and sequencing of visual operations is also important. Therefore the approach taken in this book is functional and modular. Specific brain structures are mentioned because each has a specialized function in the visual thinking process. We could just talk about these brain structures as abstract functioning modules, but giving them their proper names preserves the link with the underlying science. Overall the goal is to steer a path between oversimplification and overwhelming neurophysiological detail.

There is a general point to be considered regarding the modular structure of the brain. The brain is not a holistic undifferentiated processor of information, as was once thought. Instead, it is made up of a number of specialized regions, each devoted to carrying out some specific processing task, such as scheduling eye movements, or processing features. Visual thinking comes about through the coordinated activities of these processing regions. There is no central processing unit in the brain, rather the whole functions as a kind of *distributed* computer. Also, there is no central conductor coordinating all of the distributed parts. Each component coordinates interactions with the other components to which it is connected. This is the reason why we can sometimes carry out more than one task simultaneously—talking and driving a car, for example. These tasks use regions of the brain that are mostly independent.

The idea of distributed cognition is no longer particularly controversial, but the idea of distributed cognition begs to be extended outside the head, and this is truly radical. Distributed cognition holds that cognition is the result of a set of interconnected processing modules, each doing something relatively simple and sending signals on to other modules. But why must these modules be inside the head? What is the difference between information stored in human memory, and information stored in a book, or picture? After all, we can store images in a photo album far better than we can store them in our head. We can store them even better on a computer if it has an effective search capability. Thinking involves a constant interplay between new patterns and old patterns, and patterns can come from both inside and outside the skull. As Don Norman famously noted, *"The power of the unaided mind is highly overrated. Without external aids, memory, thought and reasoning are all constrained. But human intelligence is highly flexible and adaptive, superb at inventing procedures and objects that overcome its own limits. The real powers come from devising external aids that enhance cognitive activities. How have we increased memory, thought and reasoning? By the invention of external aids: it is things that make us smart"* (Norman 1993).

Graphs, diagrams, and illustrations have only become widely available as visual thinking tools over the past 200 years. More recently there has been an explosive development of diagramming techniques driven first by color printing technology and currently by the Internet. Graphic PowerPoint♦ slides and the like have become a ubiquitous tool for information presentation. Increasingly, the tools that support cognition are computer-based, and increasingly they incorporate images and visualizations as well as words. The term *visualization* as it is used in the previous sentence is actually quite new. Visualizations used to be mental images that people formed while they thought. Now the term more often means a graphical representation of some data or concepts. Visualizations are becoming important in most areas of science and commerce.

♦PowerPoint is a product of Microsoft Corporation.

Advertisements have long been visualizations. All of these artifacts are tools for visual thinking.

When visualizations are used in presentations, they can provide a medium whereby the executable mental models of those in the audience can be modified. According to the theory of predictive cognition, which forms the basis of Chapter 8, memories are better understood as a system of executable mental models of the world and our place in it, not as inert repositories. The goal of communication is to support the transmission of better mental models so that individuals can think and act better.

CONCLUSION

Perceiving is a skilled active process. We seek out what we need through frequent eye movements, so that critical information falls on the high-resolution fovea. Eye movements are executed to satisfy our need for information and can be thought of as a sequence of visual queries on the visual world. Each time the eye briefly comes to rest, the pattern-processing machinery goes to work sorting out what is most likely to be relevant to our current cognitive task. Almost everything else is either not seen at all or retained for only a fraction of a second. A few fragments are held for a second or two, and a tiny percentage forms part of our long-term memory. To be sure, we do have visual memories built up over our lifetimes and these are what make the scraps of information we capture meaningful and useful. These memories are not detailed, but they do provide frameworks for fleshing out the fragments. They also provide frameworks for planning eye movements and other kinds of actions.

The idea of the visual query is shorthand for what we do when we obtain information either from the world at large or some kind of information display. We make visual queries every time we search for some visual information that we need to carry out our cognitive task of the moment. Understanding what visual queries are easily executed is a critical skill for the designer. The special skill of designers is not so much skill with drawing or graphic design software, although these are undoubtedly useful, but the talent to analyze a design in terms of its ability to support the visual queries of others. This talent comes from hard-won pattern analysis skills that become incorporated into the neural fabric of perception, as well as the skill to execute a cognitive process that takes into account a variety of competing considerations.

One reason design is difficult is that the designer already has the knowledge expressed in the design, has seen it develop from inception, and therefore cannot see it with fresh eyes. The solution is to be analytic and this is where this book is intended to have value. Effective design should start with a visual task analysis, determine the set of visual queries to be supported by a design, and then use color, form and space to efficiently serve those queries. Skilled graphic designers already do this intuitively. It is my earnest hope that this book will help in the transition from unskilled to skilled designer by providing visual analytic tools derived from an up-to-date understanding of human perception.

At this stage, it should be clear that this book is not about the kind of visual thinking that goes into fine art where the goals are frequently the opposite of clarity, but rather beauty, visual impact, or an investigation of a new vocabulary of expression. Because of its exploratory, pioneering nature, leading-edge art often speaks only to small cliques of insiders, collectors, critics, and gallery owners. This book is about graphic design that provides a channel for clear communication that supports visual thinking and acts as an interface to the vast information resources of the modern world. This should not, however, imply that its message is the enemy of creative expression. There is never a single optimal solution to a design problem, but rather a huge variety of alternative clear and effective designs.

Chapter 2

What We Can Easily See

Imagine a thief searching a moonlit room with a flashlight. He can see the vague outlines of furniture but no details at all. He uses the narrow beam of the flashlight to pick out the tops of dressers and side tables where he expects valuables may be. Our visual attention actually works something like this: we move the spotlight of our attention by moving our eyes from point to point, picking out details. Generally we only have vague information to plan each eye movement, so we often fail to find the information we seek on a particular eye fixation. But some things are very easy to find even at the edge of the visual field, like a blinking light over the water or a bright patch of red sweater in a crowd of people wearing black. We can sense them in the periphery and then make an eye movement so that they become the center of both vision and attention.

This chapter is about the theory of vision that describes what makes something small easy to see. It is also about the nitty-gritty details of design. What does it take to make a graphic symbol that can be found rapidly? How can

Visual Thinking for Information Design. DOI: https://doi.org/10.1016/B978-0-12-823567-6.00002-1

something be highlighted? The problem for the designer is to ensure all visual queries can be effectively and rapidly served. In practice, this means ensuring that semantically meaningful graphic objects that make up a design each have the right amount of salience. The most important and frequent visual queries should be supported with the most visually distinct objects. The perceptual laws of visual distinctness are based on the low-level early-stage processing in the visual system. The elementary pattern-processing systems we find there provide the substrate on which all graphical interpretation is built.

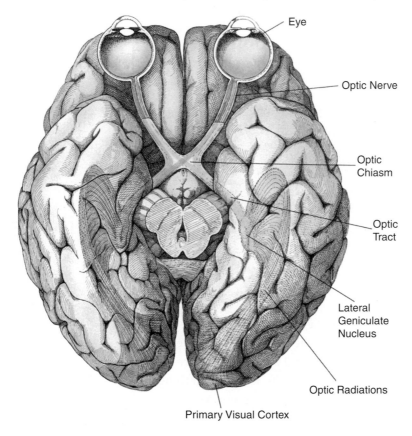

Eye

Optic Nerve

Optic Chiasm

Optic Tract

Lateral Geniculate Nucleus

Optic Radiations

Primary Visual Cortex

A view of the brain from beneath. Light is transformed into neural signals by the retina. Information is then passed along the optic nerve, via the waystation of the lateral geniculate nucleus to the primary visual cortex located at the back of the brain.

In the primary visual cortex billions of neurons process the entire image, providing the elements of form, color, texture, stereoscopic depth, and motion all at once.

In the following set of random letters, two p's have been highlighted with a yellow background. Finding those two p's is easy. They seem to pop out from the page. In contrast, it is more difficult to find the two q's. To find the q's, every letter must be scanned and it will take at least ten times longer than finding the p's. Further, finding the q's will impose a much greater cognitive burden, certainly disrupting one's train of thought.

ehklhfdiyaiorywekⅼblkhockxlyhirhupwerlkhlkuyxoiasusifdh
lksajdhflkihqdaklljerlajesljselusdslfjsalsuslcjlsdsjaf;ljdulafjluj
oufojrtopjhklghqlkshlkfhlkdshflymcvciwopzlsifhrmckreieui

The fact that the p's are easy to see seems straightforward and unsurprising. But why do the q's take longer to find? After all, we all spend thousands of hours reading and writing with this alphabet. So the q shape is not unfamiliar.

THE MACHINERY OF LOW-LEVEL FEATURE ANALYSIS

In order to understand why the p's are easy and the q's are hard on the preceding image, we need to dig more deeply into what is going on during the earlier stages of visual processing. The neural architecture of the primary visual cortex has been mapped in detail through experiments in which neurophysiologists inserted very small electrical probes into single neurons in the brains of various animals. David Hubel and Torsten Weisel pioneered this method in the 1960s. They discovered that at the back of the brain in a region called the primary visual cortex (also called visual area 1, or V1), cells would "fire," thereby emitting a series of spikes of electrical current when certain kinds of patterns were put in front of an animal's eyes.[*] Through many hundreds of such experiments, neuroscientists have discovered that V1 is a kind of tapestry of interlocking regions where different kinds of information are processed. The elements of color, shape, texture, motion, and stereoscopic depth are processed by different interwoven areas. Visual area 2 (V2) receives input from V1. V2's neurons respond to slightly more complex patterns, based on the processing already done in V1.

[*]David Hubel and Torsten Wiesel obtained a Nobel Prize for this groundbreaking research in 1981.

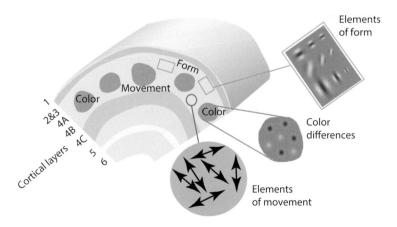

Elements of form

Color differences

Elements of movement

Form

Movement

Color

Color

Cortical layers

1
2&3
4A
4B
4C
5
6

A fold of the primary visual cortex (V1) contains many layers of neurons. Signals from the retina, via the lateral geniculate nucleus, come up through several layers, dense with cross connections to layers 3 and 4 where individual neurons each respond to a specific simple feature.

There are a million nerve fibers providing input from each eye to the V1 area where several billion neurons process information. Information is then passed on to area V2 where several billion more neurons process it at a more complex level. Areas V1 and V2 can each be thought of as a parallel computer, far more complex and powerful than anything humans have built to date. Parallel computing is the name given to computer systems that are made up of many small computers each doing essentially the same thing on a different piece of data. These kinds of computers are used to solve problems such as weather forecasting, where each processor deals with a little bit of the atmosphere. These cortical areas are *parallel* computers because they process every part of the visual image simultaneously, computing local orientation information, local color difference information, local size information, and local motion information.

WHAT AND WHERE PATHWAYS

In this chapter, we are mostly concerned with what goes on in the primary visual cortex, but it is useful to look ahead a bit and see where the information is going. V1 and V2 provide the inputs to two distinct processing systems called the *what* and the *where* systems, respectively.◆

◆Area V3 is also part of both what and where pathways, but its processing role is still uncertain.

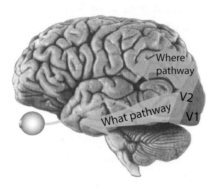

The what pathway sweeps forward from V1 and V2 along the lower edge of the brain on each side, processing information about the identity of an object.

The where pathway sweeps forward higher up on the brain and processes information about where objects in the world are located.

The what pathway is concerned with the identification of objects in the environment. It helps identify if a particular pattern of light and color represents a chicken, a Volkswagen, or Aunt Mabel. The where pathway is concerned with the location of information and with guiding actions in the world, such as reaching out and grabbing things, moving from place to place or making eye movements. What makes an object easy to find is how easily we can direct a rapid eye movement to focus our attention on it.

EYE MOVEMENT PLANNING

Visual search is not random; however, there is a chicken and egg problem. If we are looking for something smallish, we can only see it when we are looking at it. But how do the eyes get directed to the right locations if the information has not been processed? The answer is that there is very limited preprocessing that is used to direct attention. To understand this is to understand what is easy to see.◆

◆The theory of visual search presented here is from J.M. Wolf and T.S. Horowitz, 2004. What attributes guide the deployment of visual attention and how do they do it? *Nature Reviews Neuroscience.* 5(6): 495–501.

Part of the machinery is a mechanism called *biased competition*. If we are looking for tomatoes, then it is as if an instruction has been issued. "All you red-sensitive cells in V1, you all have permission to shout louder. All you blue- and green-sensitive cells, be quiet." Similar instructions can be issued for particular orientations, or particular sizes—these are all features processed by V1. The responses from the cells that are thereby sensitized are passed both up the *what* pathway biasing the things that are seen, and up the *where* pathway, to regions that send signals to make eye movements occur. Other areas buried deeper in the brain, such as the hippocampus, are also involved in setting up actions.

In a search for tomatoes, all red patches in the visual field of the searcher become candidates for eye movements, and the one that causes red-sensitive neurons to shout the loudest will be visited first. The same biased shouting mechanism also applies to any of the feature types processed by the primary visual cortex, including orientation, size, and motion. The important point here is that knowing what the primary visual cortex does tells us what is easy to find in a visual search.

This is by no means the whole story of eye-movement planning. Prior knowledge about where things are will also determine where we will look. However, in the absence of prior knowledge, understanding what will stand out on a poster, or computer screen, is largely about the kinds of features that are processed early on, before the where and what pathways diverge.

WHAT STANDS OUT = WHAT WE CAN BIAS FOR

Some things seem to *pop out* from the page at the viewer. It seems you could not miss them if you tried. For example **Anne** *Triesman* name almost certainly popped out at you the moment you turned to this page. Anne Triesman is the psychologist who was the first to systematically study the properties of simple patterns that made them easy to find. Triesman carried out dozens of experiments on our ability to see simple colored shapes as distinct from other shapes surrounding them.[*]

[*]A large number of pop-out experiments are summarized in A. Triesman and S. Gormican, 1988. Feature analysis in early vision: Evidence from search asymmetries. *Psychological Review*. 95(1): 15–98.

Triesman's experiments consisted of visual search tasks. Subjects were first told what the target shape was going to be and given an instant to look at it; for example, they were told to look for a tilted line. ╲

Next they were briefly exposed to that same shape embedded in a set of other shapes called distracters.

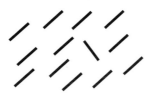

They had to respond by pressing a "yes" button if they saw the shape, and a "no" button if they did not see it. In some trials, the shape was present, and in others it was not.

The critical finding was that for certain combinations of targets and distracters the time to respond *did not* depend on the number of distracters. The shape was just as distinct and the response was just as fast if there were a hundred distracters as when there was only one. This suggests a parallel automatic process. Somehow all those hundred things were being eliminated from the search as quickly as one. Triesman claimed that the effects being measured by this method were *pre-attentive.* That is, they occurred because of automatic mechanisms operating prior to the action of attention and taking advantage of the parallel computing of features that occurs in V1 and V2.

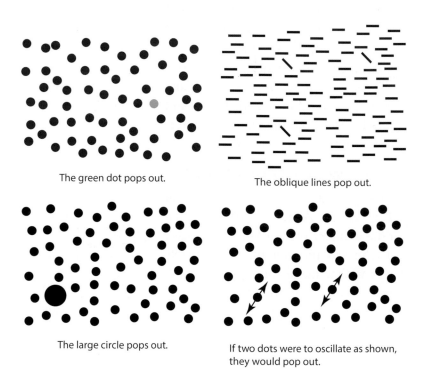

The green dot pops out.

The oblique lines pop out.

The large circle pops out.

If two dots were to oscillate as shown, they would pop out.

Pop-out effects depend on the relationship of a visual search target to the other objects that surround it. If that target is distinct in some feature channel of the primary visual cortex, we can program an eye movement so that it becomes the center of fixation.

Although these studies have contributed enormously to our understanding of early-stage perceptual processes, pre-attentive has turned out to be an unfortunate choice of term. Intense concentrated attention is required for the kinds of experiments Triesman carried out, and her subjects were all required to *focus their attention on the presence or absence of a particular target.* They were paid to attend as hard as they could. More recent experiments where subjects were not told of the target ahead of time show that all except the most blatant targets are missed.[*] To be sure, some things shout so loudly that they pop out whether we want them to or not. A bright flashing light is an example. But most of the visual search targets that Triesman used would not have been seen if subjects had not been told what to look for, and this is why pre-attentive is a misnomer.

A better term would be *tunable*, to indicate those visual properties that can be used in the planning of the next eye movement. Triesman's experiments tell us about those kinds of shapes that have properties to which our eye-movement programming system is sensitive. These are the properties that guide the visual search process and determine what we can easily see.

The strongest pop-out effects occur when a single target object differs in some feature from all other objects and where all the other objects are identical, or at least very similar to one another. Visual distinctness has as much to do with the visual characteristics of the *environment* of an object as the characteristics of the object itself. It is the degree of feature-level *contrast* between an object and its surroundings that make it distinct. For the purposes of understanding pop-out, contrast should be defined in terms of the basic features that are processed in the primary visual cortex. The simple features that lead to pop-out are color, orientation, size, motion, and stereoscopic depth. There are some exceptions, such as convexity versus concavity of contours that pop out to a lesser extent. These are somewhat mysterious, because primary visual cortex neurons have not yet been found that respond to these properties. But generally there is a striking correspondence between pop-out effects and the early processing mechanisms.

Something that pops out can be seen in a single eye fixation, and experiments show that processing to separate a pop-out object from its surroundings actually takes less than a tenth of a second. Things that do not pop out usually require several eye movements to find, with eye movements taking place at a rate of roughly three per second. Between one and a few seconds may be needed for a search. These may seem like small differences, but they represent the difference between visually efficient at-a-glance processing and cognitively effortful search.

So far we have only looked at patterns that show the pop-out effect. But what patterns *do not* show pop-out? It is equally instructive to examine these. On the following page, there is a box containing a number of red and green squares and circles. When you turn the page, look for the green squares in the figure at the top of the facing page.

[*]The phenomenon of not seeing things that should be obvious is called inattentional blindness. A. Mack and I. Rock, 1998. *Inattentional Blindness*. MIT Press, Cambridge, MA.

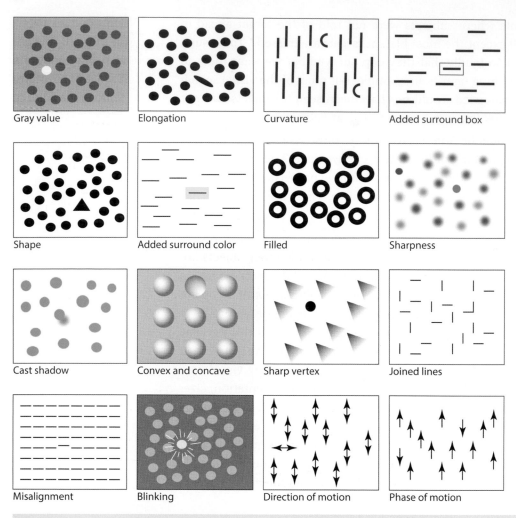

Gray value

Elongation

Curvature

Added surround box

Shape

Added surround color

Filled

Sharpness

Cast shadow

Convex and concave

Sharp vertex

Joined lines

Misalignment

Blinking

Direction of motion

Phase of motion

What makes a feature distinct is that it differs from the surrounding feature in terms of the signal it provides to the low-level feature-processing mechanisms of the primary visual cortex.

Trying to find a target based on a combination of two features (square and green on the facing page) is called a visual conjunctive search, and most visual conjunctions are hard to see. Neurons sensitive to more complex conjunction patterns are only found further up the *what* processing pathway, and these cannot be used to plan eye movements. In each of the following examples, there is something that is easy to find and something that is not easy to find. The easy-to-find things can be differentiated by V1 neurons. The hard-to-find things can only be differentiated by neurons further up the what pathway.

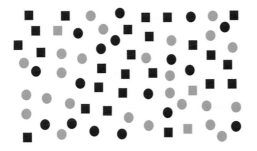

There are three green squares in this pattern. The green squares do not show a pop-out effect, even though you know what to look for. The problem is that your primary visual cortex can either be tuned for the square shapes, or the green things, but not both.

For the pop-out effect to occur, it is not enough that low-level feature differences simply exist, they must also be sufficiently large. For example, as a rule of thumb a 30-degree orientation difference is needed for a feature to stand out. The extent of variation in the background is also important. If the background is extremely homogenous, for example, a page of twelve-point text, then a small difference is needed to make a particular feature distinct. The more the background varies *in a particular feature channel*—such as color, texture, or orientation—then the larger the difference required to make a feature distinct.

We can think of the problem of seeing an object clearly in terms of *feature channels.* Channels are defined by the different ways the visual image

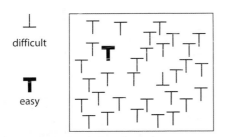

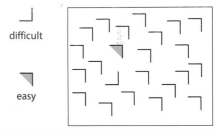

The inverted T has the same feature set as the right-side-up T and is difficult to see. But the bold T does support pop-out and is easy to find.

Similarly, the backward L has the same feature set as the other items making it difficult to find. But the green triangle addition does pop out.

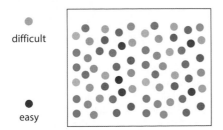

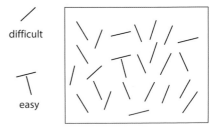

A color that is close to many other similarly colored dots cannot be tuned for and is difficult to find.

Similarly, if a line is surrounded by other lines of various similar orientations, it will not stand out.

is processed in the primary visual cortex. Feature channels provide a useful way of thinking about what makes something distinct. The following diagrams each represent two feature channels. You can think of one axis representing the color channel and the other axis representing the size channel. The circle represents a target symbol having a particular color and size. This is what is being searched for. The filled circles represent all of the other features on the display.

Objects to be searched

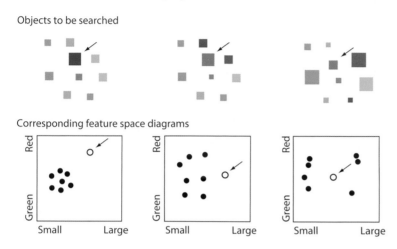

Corresponding feature space diagrams

TOP ROW. Three sets of objects to be searched. In each case an arrow shows the search target. BOTTOM ROW. The corresponding feature space diagrams. If a target symbol differs on two feature channels, it will be more distinct than if it differs only on one. On the left panel the target differs in both color and size from non-targets. In the middle panel the target differs only in size from non-targets. A target will be least distinct if it is completely surrounded in feature space as is shown in the right panel.

One might think that finding things quickly is simply a matter of practice and we could learn to find complex patterns rapidly if we practiced enough. The fact is that learning does not help much. Visual learning is

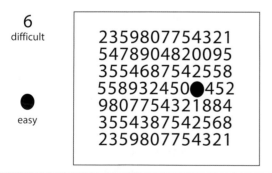

The number 6 cannot be picked out from all the other numbers despite a lifetime's experience looking at numbers; searching for it will take about 2 seconds. By contrast the dot can be seen in a single glance, about ten times faster. The features that pop out are hardwired in the brain, not learned.

Individual faces also do not pop out from the crowd even though it may be our brother or sister we are looking for. However, the pinkish round shapes of faces in general may be tunable, and so our visual systems can program a series of eye movements to faces. This does not help much in this picture because there are so many faces. The yellow jacket in the image on the right can be found with a single fixation because there is only one yellow object and no other similar colors.

a valuable skill and with practice experts can interpret patterns that non-experts fail to see. But this expertise applies more to identifying patterns once they have been fixated with the eyes, and not to finding those patterns out of the corner of the eye.

LESSONS FOR DESIGN

The lessons from these examples are straightforward. If you want to make something easy to find, make it different from its surroundings according to some primary visual channel. Give it a color that is substantially different from all other colors on the page. Give it a size that is substantially different from all other sizes. Make it a curved shape when all other shapes are straight; make it the only thing blinking or moving, and so on.

Many design problems, however, are more complex. What if you wish to make several things easily searchable at the same time? The solution is to use different *channels*. As we have seen, layers in the primary visual cortex are divided up into small areas that *separately* process the elements of form (most importantly, orientation and size), color, and motion. These can be thought of as semi-independent processing channels for visual information.

A design to support a rapid visual query for two different attributes of symbols from will be most effective if each kind of query uses a different channel. Suppose we wish to understand how gross domestic product (GDP) relates to education, population growth rates, and city dwelling for a sample of countries. Only two of these variables can be shown on a conventional scatter plot, but the others can be shown using shape and color. We plot the GDP against population growth rate, and we use shape coding for literacy and color coding for urbanization.

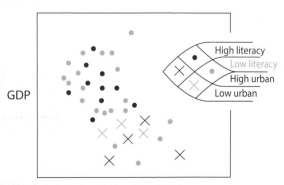

Population Growth Rate

In this scatter plot, two different kinds of points are easy to find. It is easy to visually query those data points representing countries with a high level of literacy. These use color coding. It is also easy to visually query the set of points representing countries with a low urban population. These are distinct on the orientation channel because these symbols are made with ✕s containing strong oblique lines.

It is not necessary to restrict ourselves to a single channel for each kind of symbol. If there are differences between symbols on multiple channels, they will be even easier to find. Also, tunability is not an all-or-nothing property of graphic symbols. A symbol can be made to stand out in only a single feature channel. For example, the size channel can be used to make a symbol distinct, but if the symbol can be made to differ from other symbols in both size and color, it will be even more distinct.

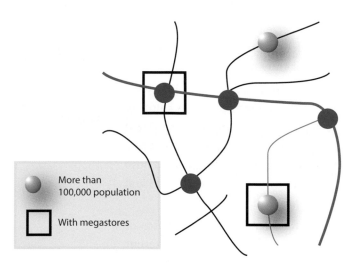

More than
100,000 population

With megastores

Suppose that we wish to display both large towns and towns with megastores on the same map. Multiple tunable differences can be used. The blue symbols are shaded in 3D and have cast shadows. The outline squares are constructed from the only bold straight vertical and horizontal lines on the map. This means that visual queries for either large towns or towns with megastores will be efficiently queried.

Any complex design will contain a number of background colors, line densities, and textures, and the symbols will similarly differ in size, shape, color, and texture. It is a challenge to create a design having more than

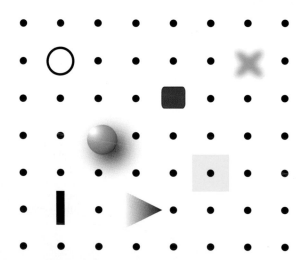

A set of symbols designed so that each would be independently searchable.

Each symbol differs from the others on several channels. For example, there is only one green symbol; it is the only one with oblique lines and it is the only one with no sharp edges.

two or three symbols so that each one will support rapid pop-out searching. Creating a display containing more than eight to ten *independently* searchable symbols is probably impossible simply because there are not enough channels available. When we are aiming for pop-out, we only have about three difference steps available on each channel: three sizes, three orientations, three frequencies of motion, etc. The following set is an attempt to produce seven symbols that are as distinct as possible given that the display is static.

There is an inherent tradeoff between stylistic consistency and overall clarity that every designer must come to terms with. The seven different symbols are stylistically very different from each other. It is easy to construct a stylistically consistent symbol set using either seven different colors or seven different shapes, but there is a cognitive cost in doing so. Visual searches will take longer if only color coding is used, than when shape, texture, and color differentiate the symbols, and in a complex display the difference can be extreme. What takes a fraction of a second with the multi-feature design might easily take several seconds with the consistent color-only design.

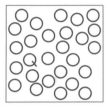

Many kinds of visibility enhancements are not symmetric. Increasing the size of a symbol will result in something that is more distinctive than a corresponding decrease in size. Similarly, an increase in contrast will be more distinctive than a decrease in contrast. Adding an extra part to a symbol is more distinctive than taking a part away.

There is a kind of visual competition in the street as signs compete for our attention.

Blinking signs are the most effective in capturing our attention. When regulation allows it and budgets are unlimited, Times Square is the result.

36

MOTION

Making objects move is a method of visibility enhancement that is in a class by itself. If you are resting on the African Savannah, it pays to be sensitive to motion at the edge of your visual field. That shaking of a bush seen out of the corner of your eye might be the only warning you get that something is stalking you with lunch in mind. The need to detect predators has been a constant factor through hundreds of millions of years of evolution, which presumably explains why we and other animals are extremely sensitive to motion in the periphery of our visual field. Our sensitivity to *static* detail falls off very rapidly away from the central fovea. Our sensitivity to motion falls off much less, so we can still see that something is moving out of the corner of our eye, even though the shape is invisible.

Motion is extremely powerful in generating an *orienting response*. It is hard to resist looking at an icon jiggling on a web page, which is exactly why moving icons can be irritating. A study by A.P. Hillstrom and S. Yantis suggests that the things that most powerfully elicit the orienting response are not simply things that move, but things that *emerge* into the visual field.[*] We rapidly become habituated to simple motion; otherwise, every blade of grass moving would startle us.

*A.P. Hillstrom and S. Yantis, 1994. Visual attention and motion capture. *Perception and Psychophysics.* 55(4): 109–154.

In the design of computer interfaces, one good use of motion is as a kind of human interrupt. Sometimes people wish to be alerted to incoming email or instant messaging requests. Perhaps in the future virtual agents will scour the Internet for information and occasionally report back their findings. Moving icons can signal their arrival. If the motion is rapid, the effect may be irritating and hard to ignore, and this would be useful for urgent messages. If the motion is slower and smoother, the effect can be a gentler reminder that there is something needing attention. Of course, if we want to use the emergence of an object to provoke an orienting response on the part of the computer user, it is not enough to have something emerge only once. We do not see things that change when we are in the midst of making an eye movement or when we are concentrating. Signaling icons should emerge then disappear every few seconds or minutes to reduce habituation.[*]

*I introduced the idea of using motion as a human interrupt in a paper I wrote with collaborators in 1992. C. Ware, J. Bonner, W. Knight, and R. Cater. Moving icons as a human interrupt. *International Journal of Human-Computer Interaction.* 4(4): 173–178.

The web designer now has the ability to create web pages that crawl, jiggle, and flash. Unsurprisingly, because it is difficult for people to suppress the orienting response to motion, this has provoked a strong aversion among users to the websites where these effects flourish. The gratuitous use of motion is one of the worst forms of visual pollution, but carefully applied motion can be a useful technique. This is not to say that motion per se is bad. We can be outdoors where trees sway, clouds move, and people pass to and fro without feeling irritated. It is especially high-frequency rapid motion or blinking that induces the unavoidable orienting response. Another caveat with respect to motion is that many people like the energy and stimulation that motion imparts—one person's amusement arcade is another person's hell. We should make the distinction between situations where the goal is entertainment and situations where the goal is providing information in the most effective possible way.

VISUAL SEARCH STRATEGIES AND SKILLS

So far we have focused on the specific feature properties that are used in the very short-term planning of the next eye movement, but this is by no means the whole story. Finding a small object is a skilled strategic process. At every instant in time, part of the brain is planning the next eye movement based on the information available from the current fixation of the eye as well as some small amount that is retained from the previous few fixations. Visual search is a prime example of how *executable memories* operate as introduced in Chapter 1. Our neurally encoded experience tells us where to look for something and this knowledge is stored as a pattern of eye movement tendencies. The brain predicts the outcome of eye movements and as a visual search proceeds, and the search plan is adapted based on whether or not predicted outcomes occur. If we find something we are looking for we stop, or we may find additional information that increased our chances of finding what we want on the next fixation. The way that experience with similar visual environments influences the visual search pattern is part of the skill of visual thinking. When we read a newspaper, for example, we are likely to scan the main headlines and images first. But the patterns of eye movements that occur in response to a particular scene are never inevitable; it is a fluid just-in-time process, and the potential search targets are continually being reassessed.

A graphic design that has visual structure at several scales can aid the search process. Large-scale structure is needed as a means for finding important mid-scale and small-scale information.

THE DETECTION FIELD

Remember that the size of processing units (brain pixels) increases with distance from the center of gaze (see Chapter 1). Small features cannot be detected by large brain pixels at the edge of visual space. If the targets are small and near the current center of fixation, the brain can apply the selective feature-based biasing mechanism we have been discussing. But if small targets are off to the side, some other process must kick in. Several

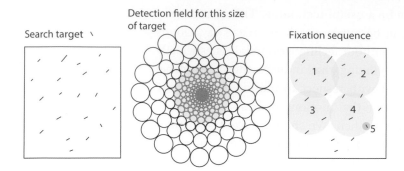

Search target

Detection field for this size of target

Fixation sequence

Brain pixels get larger the further away they are from the point of fixation, thus several eye movements are needed before the target can be detected. On the fourth fixation, the target is detected at the edge of the tunable region. A final eye movement brings it to the center of the fovea.

eye movements will be required to scan the visual field until one lands close enough to the target.

The area around the center of the fovea where the presence of a particular target may be detected can be thought of as a *detection field*. If a search target is within the detection field, this does not necessarily mean that it can be positively identified; it only means that this can become a target for the next fixation, and after that it may be identified. One of the skills of seeing is a set of neurally encoded *scanning strategies*. A typical scanning strategy is the one we use when reading; we start in the upper left-hand corner and move our eyes across from left to right, starting at the top and progressing down. In most real-world search tasks, the visual field is not uniformly filled with potential candidates and part of a scanning strategy is to get the eye *in the vicinity* of the target so that the feature-based pop-out mechanism can function as a final step. Supporting this can improve visualization designs.

Sometimes the likely candidates are grouped in clusters, and our search strategy will take advantage of this. Big patterns have a much bigger detection field, and this allows for a hierarchical search strategy. If small target patterns are embedded in specific types of large patterns, then this information can be used. First we make an eye movement to the likely neighborhood of a target, based on the limited information in our peripheral vision; next, the local pattern information provides a few candidates for individual detailed fixations.

Our everyday environment has structure at all scales. Rooms contain large furniture objects such as desks, chairs, bookshelves, and cupboards, as well as small hand-sized objects such as books, telephones, and coffee cups. These are arranged in predictable relationships; the books are on the shelves and the desktops, and the coffee cup is on the desk. This allows for a much more efficient visual search. For the thief in the night, the big patterns may be dressers and side tables. The small patterns may be pieces of jewelry. Sometimes it can be enough that the small targets are arranged in clumps, enabling a strategy based on looking first for the clumps, then searching within each clump.

Ultimate target    First search targets   Fixation sequence

In this example, the targets are clustered and a two-stage search strategy is used. The first stage involves tuning for and making an eye movement to a cluster of targets (seen as fuzzy blobs in the periphery). After the fixation is made, the blob is resolved into individual targets. The second stage involves tuning for and making an eye movement to a particular candidate target within a blob. The final tuning is based on orientation.

The process we have described so far is missing one essential property. How does the search control system avoid revisiting places that have already been examined? Even the best scanning strategy can fail and unless there is a memory for where eye fixations have recently been placed, the point just visited will be the best candidate for the next fixation. Without a blocking mechanism the eye would be trapped, flicking back and forth between the two most likely target areas. The brain must somehow mark the locations of recent fixations and inhibit the tendency to revisit them. It is thought that a structure on the *where* pathway called the *lateral interparietal* area performs this function.[*] Experimental evidence suggests that between four and six locations recently visited with eye movements are retained. In some cases, the identity of the object at a particular location may also be retained in visual working memory, but in other cases the brain simply flags the fact that a particular location has been visited.

[*]See J.W. Bisley and M.E. Goldberg, 2003. Neuronal activity in the lateral interparietal area and spatial attention. *Science.* 299: 81–86.

THE VISUAL SEARCH PROCESS

We can now elaborate on the inner loops of visual problem solving that were introduced in Chapter 1, concentrating on the eye-movement control process. We will start with the outermost loop and work in.

Move-and-scan loop. Assuming that we know what we are looking for, when we enter an environment, our initial search strategy will involve orienting the head and perhaps walking to get the best viewpoint based on our executable memories of that kind of environment. From this vantage, we will initiate a sequence of fixations. If the target is not found, we move to a new vantage point to continue the search.

Eye-movement control loop. Planning and executing eye movements occurs between one and three times per second. This involves both the biasing mechanism, so that new candidate targets can be determined based on their elementary properties of form (orientation, size, color, motion), and a simple map of what regions have been recently visited by means of eye movements.

Pattern-testing loop. When the eye alights on a promising target area, the inner loop function is executed. This involves testing the pattern to see if it is the search target or not. The brain takes about one-twentieth of a second to make each test; typically between one and four tests are made on each fixation.

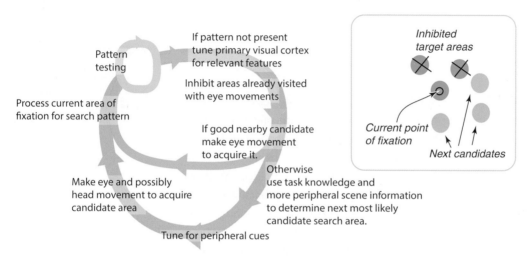

USING MULTISCALE STRUCTURE TO DESIGN FOR SEARCH

To support efficient visual search, a design should be given large-scale as well as small-scale structure. All too often, artificial information displays lack visual structure at different scales. Menus and windows tend to all look the same. One rectangular box is much like another. Adding multiscale visual structure will make search much more efficient, as long as the smaller objects of search can predictably be associated with larger visual objects.

Multiscale structure

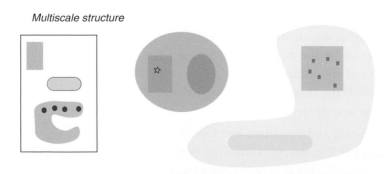

Having structure at multiple scales is most important for designs that will be used over and over again. It permits visual search skills to develop in the form of eye movement sequences that occur in response to the general properties of a particular scene. But even for designs that are used only for a few minutes, high-level structure supports location memory and makes it easier to revisit places that have been looked at only seconds ago.

CONCLUSION

Visual search is not an occasional activity only occurring when we have lost something. Because we have so little information about the immediate visual environment stored in our heads, search is something that is fundamental to almost all seeing. Even though we are mostly unaware that we are doing it, the visual world is being reassessed in terms of where we should look next on every fixation. Two seconds is a long time in a visual thinking. There is a world of difference between something that can be located with a single eye movement, and one that takes five or ten. In the former case, visual thinking will be fluid; in the latter, it will be inefficient and frustrating.

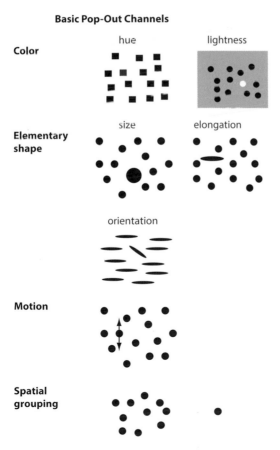

One key to making efficient visual search is through the use of pop-out properties. If a visual object is distinct on one or more of the visual channels, then it can be processed to direct an eye movement. The strongest pop-out differentiators are the basic feature channels found in V1. These include the elements of form, size, elongation, and orientation; the elements of color, including hue and lightness (these are discussed further in Chapter 4); and motion and spatial layout. The figure on the facing page gives a summary.

Large-scale graphic structure can also help with visual search, but only if the searcher *already knows* where in a large structure an important detail is likely to be. Such knowledge is built up to a limited extent as we scan a visualization, and a graphic structure is always helpful in enabling us to return to something we have recently seen. Skilled search is dependent, to a greater extent, on our previous experience with similar graphics and this is a two-edged sword. If the design being searched conforms to stereotype, then search will be easy because habitual visual scan patterns, guided by spatial structure, will support search. If a design violates a learned pattern then searches using habitual eye movement strategies will result in frustration.

Chapter 3

Structuring Two-Dimensional Space

Patterns are formed where ideas meet the evidence of the world. Top-down attentional processes cause patterns to be constructed from the retinal image that has been decomposed, like an impressionist painting, into a myriad of features in V1. Patterns are formed in a middle ground of fluid dynamic visual processing that both pulls meaningful patterns from features and imposes order based on the cognitive task of the moment. Patterns are also the building blocks of objects, which themselves can be thought of as more complex patterns.

Understanding how patterns are constructed and reconstructed can tell us a lot about the design problems of organizing space, either in ways that are unambiguous and clear, or in ways that are subject to multiple interpretations. Both have their uses. We shall start with a discussion of the dimensions of space to show why image plane patterns are so special. Then we move on to discuss how patterns are formed from the low-level features discussed in the previous chapter.

Visual Thinking for Information Design. DOI: https://doi.org/10.1016/B978-0-12-823567-6.00003-3

2.5D SPACE

Although we live in a three-dimensional world, these dimensions are not equal in terms of human perception of space. The two dimensions laid out "in the picture plane" have little in common with the third dimension toward and away from the viewpoint.

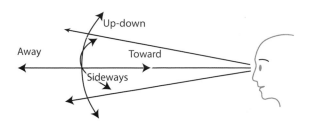

It is useful to consider visual space using radial coordinates, centered on the eye-point of an observer. We can call the three dimensions the up-down dimension, the sideways dimension, and the towards-away dimension. For convenience we shall shorten these to *up-down*, *sideways*, and *away*.

If we direct an imaginary ray away from the pupil of one of our eyes into the world, it will eventually encounter a point on the surface of an object—except for those cases when the ray reaches the empty sky. That surface point has a color and a distance from the eye. Of course, in the real world, light travels in the reverse direction and information about the surface color is recorded by cone receptors at the back of the eye, but the point is that there is only one color in the away direction corresponding to each retinal location. About a million fibers in each optic nerve transmit to the brain a million pieces of information about the world in the combined *up-down* and *sideways* dimensions (defined by the diagram above). For each of those points of information there is, at best, one additional piece of distance information relating specifically to the *away* dimension, and this extra information must be indirectly inferred. It is for this reason that people sometimes refer to visual space as having 2.5 dimensions, where the 0.5 refers to the *away* dimension. However, this substantially

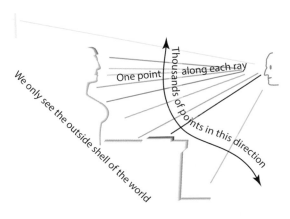

Since most things are not transparent, only facing surfaces are visible and only one point of color is available on each ray from a particular brain pixel. But there are millions of rays that can be distinguished in the up-down and sideways dimensions.

overstates the case. It would be more accurate to say that visual space has 2.05 dimensions. Sometimes the term *image plane* is used to refer to *up-down* and *sideways* dimensions combined because this is the information that can be captured on the image plane of a camera. The term *depth* is used to refer to away information.

Our ability to get a whole new sample of visual space is also radically different for the different dimensions. We can sample the *up-down* and *sideways* dimensions of space with rapid eye movements and get a mostly new sample of a million points of data on each retina in less than one-tenth of a second. By contrast, in order to get new information in the *away* direction we have to walk to a new location, so that information that was blocked becomes revealed. This can take from several seconds to a few minutes or more. Head-turning movements are intermediate in time costs and allow us to access parts of the up-down and sideways dimensions using eye movements. The point here is that image-plane sampling through eye movements is ten to a hundred times more efficient than depth sampling by walking and provides much greater cognitive efficiency.

Pattern-processing resources in the brain are mostly devoted to information in the image plane, as opposed to depth. These two-dimensional patterns are fundamentally important for two reasons. First, they are the precursors of objects. Second, a pattern can also be a relationship between objects. In some ways, pattern finding is the very essence of visual thinking, and often to perceive a pattern is to solve a problem.

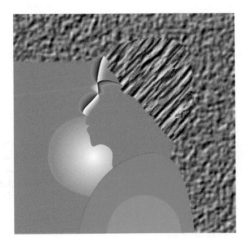

Finding the boundaries of objects is an important function of the pattern-processing systems. In order for the brain to find an object, it must somehow be distinguished from other objects in the environment, and often the most important piece of information is that it has a continuous contour running all around it. The figure on the left is distinguished from its background by many different kinds of contours.

Later in this chapter, we will examine the design implications of the brain's pattern-finding mechanisms. First, we consider how they work.

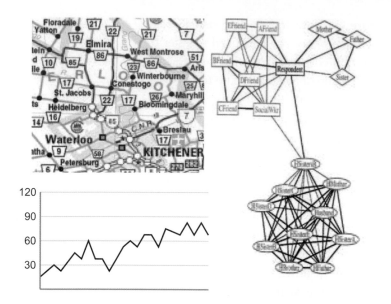

THE PATTERN-PROCESSING MACHINERY

There are two kinds of processes involved in pattern perception. One has to do with dividing up-down space through the binding of continuous contours and areas. An area called the *lateral occipital cortex* is implicated in this. The other has to do with a sequence of ever more complex patterns processed through the *what* pathway, culminating in an object.

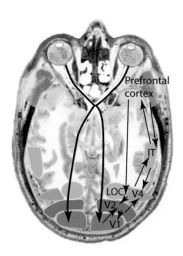

Incoming information first arrives in visual area V1 at the back of the brain. The information then passes successively through V2 and V4, and then to the inferotemporal cortex (IT). The lateral occipital cortex (LOC) is involved in region finding. Signals from the prefrontal cortex are sent back to consolidate task-relevant patterns.

This is sometimes called the "what" pathway, as opposed to the "where" pathway. The what pathway has the function of identifying objects. The where pathway has more to do with visually guided actions.

THE BINDING PROBLEM: FEATURES TO CONTOURS

We shall start with the way the brain constructs contours and areas from the millions of fragmented pieces of information in V1. The process of combining different features that will come to be identified as parts of the same contour or region is called *binding*. There is no such thing as an object embedded in an image; there are just patterns of light, shade, color, and motion. Objects and patterns must be discovered, and binding is essential because it is what makes disconnected pieces of information into connected pieces of information.*

To explain how the responses of individual feature-detecting neurons may become *bound* into a pattern representing the continuous edge of an object, let us indulge in a little anthropomorphism and imagine ourselves to be a single neuron in the primary visual cortex. As a neuron, we are far more complex than a transistor in a computer: our state is influenced by incoming signals from thousands of other neurons—some excite us, some inhibit us. When we get overexcited we *fire*, shooting a convulsive burst of electrical energy along our axon. Our outgoing axon branches out and ultimately influences the firing of thousands of other neurons. Supposing we are the kind of neuron in the primary visual cortex that responds to oriented edge information, we get most excited when part of an edge or a contour falls over a particular part of the retina to which we are sensitive. This exciting information may come from almost anything, part of the silhouette of a nose, or just a bit of oriented texture.

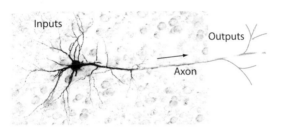

Thousands of inputs are received on the dendrites. These signals are combined in the cell body. The neuron fires an electrical spike of energy along the axon, which branches out at the end to influence other neurons, some positively, some negatively. Neurons fire all the time, and information is carried by both increases and decreases in the rate.

Now comes the interesting bit. In addition to the information from the retina, we also receive input from neighboring neurons and we set up a kind of mutual admiration society with some of them, egging them on as they egg us on. To form part of our edge-detecting club, they must respond to part of the visual world that is *in-line* with our preferred axis, and they must be attuned to roughly the same orientation. When these conditions are met, we start to pulse in unison sending out pulses of electrical energy together.

*It is never acceptable to simply say that a higher-level mechanism *looks at* the low-level information. That is called the homunculus fallacy. It is like saying that there is an inner person (a homunculus) that sees the information on the retina or in the primary visual cortex. A proper explanation is that a set of mechanisms and processes produce intelligent actions as an outcome of interactions between processes operating in sub-systems of the brain.

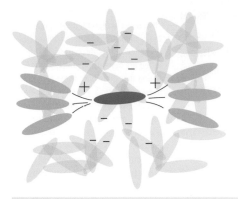

Edge detector neurons have a positive excitatory relationship with other edge detectors that are nearby and aligned. There is an inhibitory relationship with cells responding to nonaligned features.

When light from an edge falls across the receptive fields of positively connected neurons, a whole chain of neurons will start pulsing together. They are bound together by this common activity.

Our neuron is also surrounded by dozens of other neurons that respond to other orientations and, like some human groups, it actively discourages them. It sends inhibitory signals to nearby neurons that have different orientation preferences. This has the effect of damping their enthusiasm. The result is that neurons that are stimulated by long unbroken edges in the visual image mutually reinforce one another and all begin to fire in unison. Neurons responding to little fragments of edges have their signals suppressed.

A noisy edge

The response to the main contour is enhanced through mutual excitation.

The response to the short contours with other orientations is suppressed.

In addition to the signals received by the neuron from the retinal image and from its neighbors, we should not forget the top-down actions of attention. If a particular edge is part of an object that is related to some task being performed, for example, the edge belonging to the handle of a mug that someone is reaching for, then additional reinforcement and binding will occur between the pattern information and an action pattern involving the guidance of a hand. The mental act of looking for a pattern makes that pattern stand out more distinctly. On the other hand, if we are looking for a particular pattern and another pattern appears that is irrelevant to our immediate task, we are unlikely to see it.

Binding is not only something required for the edge-finding machinery. A binding mechanism is needed to account for how information stored in various parts of the brain is momentarily associated through the process of visual thinking. Visual objects that we see in our immediate environment must be temporarily bound to the information we already have stored in our brains about those objects. Also, information we gain visually must be bound to action sequences, such as patterns of eye movements, or hand movements. This higher-level binding is the subject of Chapter 6.

THE GENERALIZED CONTOUR

An object may be separated from its background in many different ways including luminance changes at its silhouette, color differences, texture boundaries, and even motion boundaries. Therefore the brain requires a generalized *contour extraction mechanism* in the pattern-processing stage of perception. Emerging evidence points to this occurring in a region called the lateral occipital cortex (LOC) that receives input from V2 and V3 allowing us to discern an object or pattern from many kinds of visual discontinuity.◆

◆Zoe Kourtzi of the University of Tuebingen in Germany and Nancy Kanwisher of MIT in the United States recently found that the lateral occipital cortex has neurons that respond to shapes irrespective of how the bounding contours are defined.

Z. Kourtzi and N. Kanwisher, 2001. Representation of perceived object shapes by the human lateral occipital cortex. *Science.* 293: 1506–1509.

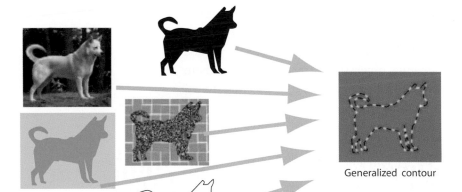

Generalized contour

Many different kinds of boundaries can activate a generalized contour.

A generalized contour does not actually look like anything. It is a pattern of neural activation in part of the brain.

One of the mysteries that is solved by the generalized contour mechanism is why line drawings are so effective in conveying different kinds of information. A pencil line is nothing like the edge of a person's face, yet a simple sketch can be instantly identifiable. The explanation of the power of lines is that they are effective in stimulating the generalized contour mechanism.

TEXTURE REGIONS

The edges of objects in the environment are not always defined by clear contours. Sometimes it is only the texture of tree bark, the pattern of leaves on the forest floor, or the way the fur lies on an animal's back that makes these things distinct. Presumably because of this, the brain also contains mechanisms that rapidly define regions having common texture and color. We shall discuss texture discrimination here. The next chapter is devoted to color.

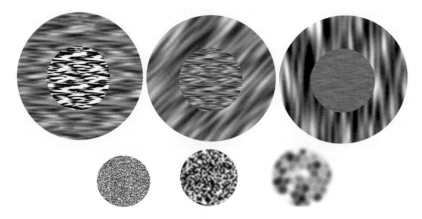

Excluding color and overall lightness, the primary factors that make one texture distinct from another are grain size, orientation, and contrast.

In general, the same properties that make individual symbols distinct (discussed in Chapter 2) will also make textures distinct. Primarily these are texture element orientation, size contrast, and color—the properties of V1 neurons in the primary visual cortex. In a way, this is hardly surprising; if large numbers of symbols or simple shapes are densely packed we stop thinking of them as individual objects and start thinking of them as a texture. The left- and right-hand sides of the texture patches shown below are *easy to discriminate* because they contain differences in how they affect neurons in the primary visual cortex.

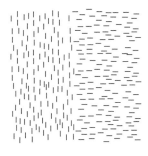

Orientation

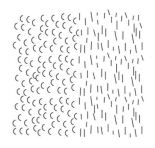

Grain size

Curve versus Straight

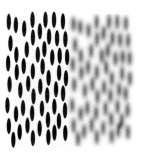

Blur

When low-level feature differences are not present in adjacent regions of texture, they are more difficult to distinguish. The following examples show *hard-to-discriminate* texture pairs.

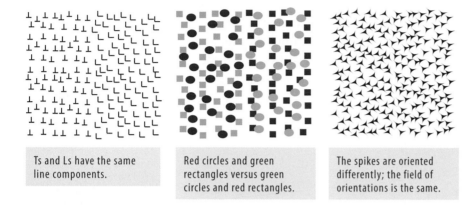

Ts and Ls have the same line components.

Red circles and green rectangles versus green circles and red rectangles.

The spikes are oriented differently; the field of orientations is the same.

Although the mechanisms that bind texture elements into regions have been studied less than the mechanisms of contour formation, we may presume that they are similar. Mutual excitation between similar features in V1 and V2 explains why we can easily see regions with similar low-level feature components through spreading activation. More complex texture patterns, such as the Ts and Ls, do not allow for the rapid segmentation of space into regions. Only basic texture differences should be used to divide space.

INTERFERENCE AND SELECTIVE TUNING

The other side of the coin of visual distinctness is visual interference. As a general rule, like interferes with like. This is easy to illustrate with text as shown here.

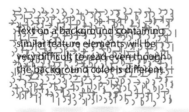

Text on a background containing similar feature elements will be very difficult to read even though the background color is different.

The more the background differs in element granularity, in feature similarity, and in the overall contrast, the easier the text will be to read.

Subtle, low contrast background texture with little feature similarity will interfere less.

To minimize this kind of visual interference (it cannot be entirely eliminated), one must maximize feature-level differences between patterns of information. Having one set of features move and another set static is probably the most effective way of separating overlaying patterns, although there are obvious reasons why doing this may not be desirable.

PATTERNS, CHANNELS, AND ATTENTION

As we discussed in Chapter 2, attentional tuning operates at the feature level, rather than the level of patterns. Nevertheless, because patterns are made up of features we can also choose to attend to particular patterns if the basic features in the patterns are different. The factors that make it easy to tune are the usual set and include color, orientation, texture, and the common motion of the elements. However, some pattern-level factors, such as the smooth continuity of contours, are also important. Once we choose to attend to a particular feature type, such as the thin red line in the illustration at the bottom of the previous page, the mechanisms that bind the contour automatically kick in.

With this figure you can choose to attend to the text, the numbers, the thin red line, or the fuzzy black symbols. As you attend to one kind of representation, the others will recede.

Representing overlapping regions is an interesting design problem that can be approached using the channel theory introduced in the previous chapter. An example problem is to design a map that shows both the mean temperature and the areas of different vegetation types. The goal is to support a variety of visual queries on the temperature zones, or the vegetation zones, or both. Applying what we know about low-level feature processing is the best way of accomplishing this. If different zones can be

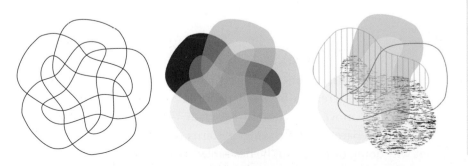

If many overlapping regions are to be shown, then a heterogeneous channel-based approach can help. On the left is a diagram in which every combination of five overlapping regions is shown. The central version using color is clearer, but still confusing. The version on the right uses color, texture, and outline. Take any point on this last diagram and it is easy to see the set of regions to which it belongs.

represented in ways that are as distinct as possible in terms of simple features, the result will be easy to interpret, although it may look stylistically muddled.

INTERMEDIATE PATTERNS

It is thought that the *what* pathway identifies objects in a series of brain regions responding to increasingly complex patterns. In area V2, neurons exist that respond to patterns only slightly more complex than the patterns found in V1 neurons. At the V4 stage, the patterns are still more complex chunks of information. V4 neurons then feed into regions in the inferotemporal (IT) cortex where specific neurons respond to images of faces, hands, automobiles, or letters of the alphabet. Each of the regions provides a kind of map of visual space that is distorted to favor central vision as discussed in Chapter 1. However, as we move up the hierarchy the mapping of visual imagery on the retina becomes less precise.

The What Hierarchy

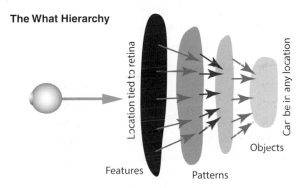

Location tied to retina

Car be in any location

Objects

Features

Patterns

As information flows up the what hierarchy, it becomes increasingly complex and tied to specific tasks, but also decreasingly localized in space. In the inferotemporal cortex, a neuron might respond to a cat anywhere in the central part of the visual field.

Currently, there is no method for directly finding out which of an infinite number of possible patterns a neuron responds to best. All researchers can do is to find, by a process of trial and error, what they respond to well. The problem increases as we move up the what hierarchy. As a result, much less is known about the mid complexity patterns of V4 than the simple ones of V1 and V2. What is known is they include patterns such as spikes, convexities, concavities, as well as boundaries between texture regions, and T and X junctions.[*] A selection is illustrated here.

[*]A. Pasupathy and C. Connor, 2002. Population coding of shape in area V4. *Nature Neuroscience.* 5(12):1332–1338.

In addition to static patterns, V4 neurons also respond well to different kinds of coherent motion patterns. Motion patterns are as important as static patterns in our interactions with the world. As we shall see in Chapter 5, motion can tell us about the layout of objects in space.

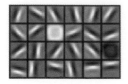  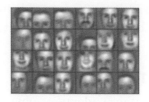

Three levels of features in a neural network trained to recognize faces.

In recent years, artificial intelligence has made great progress in using simulated, multilayer neural inspired by neuroscience. These can now often equal or exceed the performance of skilled humans in recognizing patters such as certain cancers in medical scans. Although these artificial networks differ in many respects from their biological counterparts, the patterns they learn can give us an idea what mid-level feature detectors may be like in humans and other animals. The above images show selected features at three different levels in a neural network designed to recognize faces.[•]

[•]H. Lee, R. Grosse, R. Ranganath, and A.Y. Ng, 2009, June. Convolutional deep belief networks for scalable unsupervised learning of hierarchical representations. In *Proceedings of the 26th annual International Conference on Machine Learning*. 609–616.

Motion patterns can also be especially important in telling us about the intentions of other humans and animals. Indeed there is emerging evidence that *biomotion* perception may have its own specialized pattern-detection mechanisms in the brain. We will return to this in Chapter 7, which is about language and communication.

Objects moving together are perceived as a group

PATTERN LEARNING

As we move up the processing chain, from V1 to V4 and on to the IT cortex, the effects of individual experience become more apparent[♦]. All human environments have objects with well-defined edges, and this common experience means that early in life everyone develops a set of simple oriented feature detectors in their V1. An exception to this is people with uncorrected large optical problems with their eyes when they are babies. They never learn to see detailed features, even if their eyesight is corrected optically later in life. There is a critical period in the first few years of life when the neural pattern-finding systems develop. The older we get, the worse we are at learning new patterns, and this seems to be especially true for the early stages of neural processing. There are also some differences in how much experience we have with simple patterns. A person who lives in New York City will have more cells tuned to vertical and horizontal edges than a person who exists hunting and gathering in the tangle of a rainforest. But these are relatively small differences. Leaving aside people with special visual problems, and concentrating on urban dwellers, at the level of V1 everyone is pretty much the same, and this means that design rules based on V1 properties will be universal.

One of the major breakthroughs that enabled computer AI to analyze patterns as well or better than humans was Jeff Hinton's realization that neural nets must learn low-level patterns first. Only once the basic patterns are established can the higher levels be learned. This insight came from a study of mammalian visual systems. The breakthrough is called "deep learning."

[♦]Y. LeCun, Y. Bengio, and G. Hinton, 2015. Deep learning. *Nature*. 521(7553): 436–444.

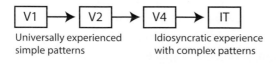

Universally experienced   Idiosyncratic experience
simple patterns   with complex patterns

The more elaborate patterns we encounter at higher levels in the visual processing chain are to a much greater extent the product of an individual's experience. There are many patterns, such as those common to faces, hands, automobiles, the characters of the alphabet, chairs, etc., that almost everyone experiences frequently, but there are also many patterns that are related to the specialized cognitive work of an individual. All visual thinking is skilled and depends on pattern learning. The map reader, the art critic, the geologist, the theatre lighting director, the restaurant chef, the truck driver, and the meat inspector have all developed particular pattern perception capabilities encoded especially in the V4 and IT cortical areas of their brains.

As an individual becomes skilled, increasingly complex patterns become encoded for rapid processing at the higher levels of the what pathway. For the beginning reader, a single fixation and a tenth of a second may be needed to process each letter shape. The expert reader will be able to capture whole words as single perceptual chunks if they are common. This gain in skill comes from developing connections in V4 neurons that transform the neurons into efficient processors of commonly seen patterns.

SERIAL PROCESSING

The pop-out effects discussed in the previous chapter are based on simple, low-level processing. More complex patterns such as those processed by levels V4 and above do not exhibit pop-out. They are processed one chunk at a time. We can take in only two or three chunks on a single fixation.

VISUAL PATTERN QUERIES AND THE APPREHENDABLE CHUNK

Patterns range from novel to those that are so well learned that they are encoded in the automatic recognition machinery of the visual system. They also range from the simple to the complex. What is of particular interest for design is the complexity of a pattern that can be apprehended in a single fixation of the eye and read into the brain in a tenth of a second or less.

Apprehendability is not a matter of size so long as a pattern can be clearly seen. For example, the green line snaking across this page can easily be apprehended in a single fixation. The visual task of finding out what lies at the end of the green line requires only a single additional eye movement once we have seen the line. But apprehendability does have to do with both complexity and interference from other patterns. Finding out if the line beginning at the red circle ends in the star shape will require a sequence of fixations. That pattern is made up of several apprehendable chunks.

For *unlearned* patterns the size of the apprehendable chunk appears to be about three feature components. Even with this simple constraint,

the variety is enormous. A few samples are given on the right to illustrate roughly the level of unlearned pattern complexity that research suggest we can take in and hold from a single glance.

MULTI-CHUNK QUERIES

Performing visual queries on patterns that are more complex than a single apprehendable chunk requires substantially greater attentional resources and a series of fixations. When the pattern is more complex than a single chunk, the visual query must be broken up into a series of subqueries, each of which is satisfied, or not, by a separate fixation. Keeping track of apprehendable chunks is the task of visual working memory, and this is a major topic of Chapter 6.

SPATIAL LAYOUT

Pattern perception is more than contours and regions. Groups of objects can form patterns based on the proximity of the elements.

Both the perception of groups and outliers are determined by proximity.

We do not need to propose any special mechanism to explain these kinds of grouping phenomena. Pattern detection mechanisms work on many scales; some neurons respond best to large shapes, others respond to smaller versions of those same shapes. A group of smaller points or objects will provoke a response from a large-shape detecting neuron, while at the same time other neurons, tuned to detect small features, respond to the individual components.

Both of the patterns shown above will excite the same large-scale feature detectors giving the overall shape. The pattern on the left will additionally stimulate small-scale detectors corresponding to the gray dots.

Large-scale oriented feature detectors will be stimulated by the large-scale structure of these patterns.

Objects in the real world have structure at many scales. In a garden, for example, individual flowers provide small-scale patterns, and these are organized into patches of color depending on the design of a flower bed. The entire structure of lawns, flower beds, trees, and paths form a large-scale pattern.

These patterns stimulate mechanisms responding to both small-scale feature and medium-scale features. They are patterns of pattern.

V4 neurons still respond strongly to patterns despite distortions that stretch or rotate the pattern, so long as the distortion is not too extreme. This is a critical property that allows us to recognize shapes and patterns even when they are seen from somewhat different angles and from somewhat different distances. A single V4 neuron might respond well to all of these different T patterns.

The ability to respond to a distorted pattern is the kind of thing that neurons do well and was difficult for computers until the advent of deep learning. It is not an exaggeration to say that our ability to perceive patterns under distortions and when partially hidden is fundamental to visual intelligence.

HORIZONTAL AND VERTICAL

The up-down direction and the sideways direction are special. They are perceived differently from each other and from other orientations. We are very sensitive to whether something is exactly vertical or horizontal and can make this judgment far more accurately than judging if a line is oriented at 45 degrees. The reason for this has to do with two things: one is maintaining our posture with respect to gravity; the other is that our modern world contains many vertically oriented rectangles and so more of our pattern-sensitive neurons become tuned to vertical and horizontal contours. This makes the vertical and horizontal organization of information an effective way of associating a set of visual objects.

The line on the right is only rotated 3 degrees from the vertical, yet this departure from parallel is clearly evident.

People are extremely sensitive when judging small end-to-end misalignments of straight lines.

PATTERN FOR DESIGN

Most designs can be considered hybrids of learned symbolic meanings, images that we understand from our experience, and patterns that visually establish relationships between the components, tying the design elements together. A design can be made visually efficient by expressing relationships by means of easily apprehended patterns.

Relationships between meaningful graphical entities can be established by any of the basic pattern-defining mechanisms we have been discussing: connecting contours, proximity, alignment, enclosing contour, color, texture, and common movement. Below are some examples of methods for establishing relationships.

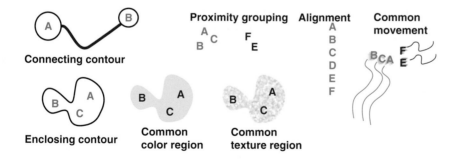

Graphic patterns defined by contour or region can be used in very abstract ways to express the structure of ideas. The relationship between concepts can be defined by graphically using techniques that are fundamental to the way diagrams work. The figure on the next page shows how *different kinds of relationships* can be established graphically.

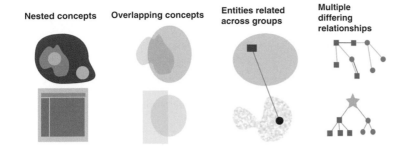

Nested concepts   Overlapping concepts   Entities related across groups   Multiple differing relationships

Relationship-defining patterns can also be used in combination. For example, a texture region can be used to define one kind of relationship, and this can be used in combination with connecting contours that define another kind of relationship. The design challenge is to use each kind of design device to its greatest advantage in providing efficient access to visual queries.

SEMANTIC PATTERN MAPPINGS

For the most part, when we see patterns in graphic designs we are relying on the same neural machinery that is used to interpret the everyday environment. There is, however, a layer of meaning—a kind of natural semantics— that is built on top of this. For example, we use a *big* graphical shape to represent a *large* quantity in a bar chart. We use something graphically attached to another object to show that it is *part of* it.

Graphical Code		Semantics
Small shapes defined by closed contour, texture, color, shaded solid.		Object, idea, entity, node.
Spatially ordered graphical objects.		Related information or a sequence. In a sequence the left-to-right ordering convention borrows from the western convention for written language.
Graphical objects in proximity.		Similar concepts, related information.
Graphical objects having the same shape, color, or texture.		Similar concepts, related information.
Size of graphical object Height of graphical object.		Magnitude, quantity, importance.

Graphical Code		Semantics
Shapes connected by contour.		Related entities, path between entities.
Thickness of connecting contour.		Strength of relationship.
Color and texture of connecting contour.		Type of relationship.
Shapes enclosed by a contour, or a common texture, or a common color.		Contained entities. Related entities.
Nested regions, partitioned regions.		Hierarchical concepts.
Attached shapes.		Parts of a conceptual structure.

These natural semantics permeate our spoken language, as well as the language of design. Indeed, the philosopher of language George Lakoff argues persuasively that spatial metaphors are not just ways of making language more vivid, they are fundamental to the way language works in communication and reasoning.[*] Even when we talk about abstract, inherently non-spatial ideas, phrases such as *connected to, built on, contained within* are so common that we do not even think of them as metaphoric. According to Lakoff, these kinds of spatial analogies are fundamental to human reasoning, which is ultimately grounded in human experience gained by interacting with the environment. Lakoff is interested in the use of spatial metaphors in natural language. Here we are concerned with *spatial metaphors* and their use in graphic design, where they are just as ubiquitous. The most basic are summarized above and on the previous page.

[*]G. Lakoff, 1980. *Metaphors We Live By*. University of Chicago Press, Chicago, IL.

EXAMPLES OF PATTERN QUERIES WITH COMMON GRAPHICAL ARTIFACTS

To elaborate these ideas, the remainder of this chapter is devoted to a set of examples of common graphical information displays. Each of them supports a form of visual reasoning; in each case the quality of the design depends on its supporting a specific set of visual pattern queries. We begin with two maps and continue with a selection of charts, a news page, and some other diagrams.

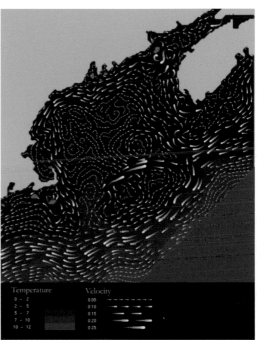

Road map. Supports route planning.

Example: Find an efficient route between Glen Allan in the upper left corner and Cambridge in the lower right. The cognitive process involves the following complex set of visual pattern queries.

Locate end points corresponding to Glen Allan and Cambridge. *[Query, visual search for text labels].*

Find path from Glen Allan to main road. *[Query, search for where gray line intersects with red line].*

Follow highway in direction of Cambridge. *[Query, visually trace red and orange lines toward the lower left].*

Detect highway exit point *[query white oval]* near to road connecting to Cambridge. At this point the point of fixation will be close enough to Cambridge that the remainder of the route can be grasped in a single apprehendable chunk.

Find path from exit to Cambridge. *[Query, discover red path from exit symbol to Cambridge symbol].*

Map of water currents and temperature. Supports reasoning about currents in the Western North Atlantic. The ocean current patterns are represented using streaklets of different length and width. The background color provides information about water temperature.

Example: Find where the strongest currents are located. *[Query, find locations of the fat long streaklets].*

Example: Find out where something that was dropped in the water (for example, fish larvae) might end up after a period of time. *[Query, find where a particular train of streaklets leads].*

Example: Find the regions with the coldest water. *[Query, find locations of darkest blue color].*

Design comment: In the regions where the current velocity is slow (thin lines), the direction is unclear.

For each example, the critical visual queries are described together with the way they are supported by the particular designs. Not all of the designs are good, and it is a useful exercise to think about how they might be improved to support the examples of visual queries. It is also a useful exercise to think about other visual thinking tasks that might be carried out with these examples, and how they might be best supported with improved designs.

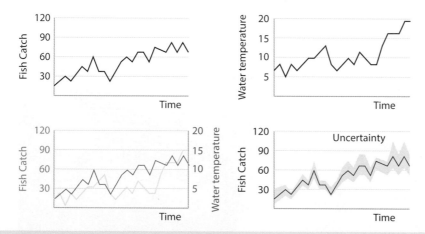

Line graph: Supports reasoning about how one measured variable changes with another.

Example: Determine fish catch as it varies over time. Common tasks are to determine when the maximum and minimum catches occurred, and whether the catch is trending up or down. *[Queries, find the highest point; find the lowest point; find whether the line slopes up or down overall.]*

Example: Often people reason by comparing one graph against another. In this case, the task might be to see if the fish catch is correlated with water temperature. *[Queries, discover if the high points and low points match for the two graphs, find if there is a correspondence in the overall trend for the two graphs.]*

Design note: Visual queries to find corresponding patterns are much easier to make if the two graphs can be combined.

Example: Often there is a degree of uncertainty in measurements, and this can be represented by a broad swath showing the uncertainty range at each point. *[Query, determine the vertical extent of the gray band at a particular point on the black line.]*

The point of the preceding examples has been to show that a wide variety of graphical display can be analyzed in terms of visual queries, each of which is essentially a visual search for a particular set of patterns. Indeed, it is a central thesis of this book that this kind of visual analysis is a critical design skill. Many of the examples can be improved, and getting into the habit of critically analyzing visualizations in terms of visual tasks is necessary for the visualization designer to develop skill.

In this chapter, we have used the term *pattern* in its everyday sense to refer to an abstract arrangement of features or shapes. There is a more general sense of the word used in cognitive neuroscience, according to which every piece of stored information can be thought of as a pattern. The sequence of processing from V1 through the IT cortex can be

Web page for news site: Supports the search for various classes of current news including business, sports, politics, etc., as well as headline stories. The page has been deliberately blurred to bring out the spatial structure.

Example: Discover major categories of news supported by this site *[query to locate top bar and left bar to find menus of alternatives]*. This design benefits from the fact that most web pages have adopted similar layout patterns.

Example: Discover current headline stories. *[Query to locate large text headlines. Read headlines. Query to locate pictures. Apprehend gist]*. The rapid apprehension of the gist of images is discussed in Chapter 5.

thought of as a series of ever more complex pattern processors, with the patterns at each level being made up of the simpler patterns processed by the preceding levels. Thus complex patterns are *patterns of patterns*.

The generalized idea of a pattern applies to more than just shapes. Temporal patterns can also be found in changing sequences of visual shapes. Behavioral responses to visual patterns can be regarded as action patterns. Finding patterns is the essence of how we make sense of the world. In a fundamental sense, the brain can be thought of as a set

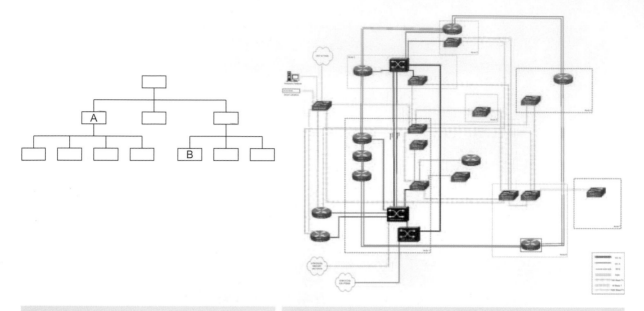

Node link diagrams: Support reasoning about relationships between entities. Typically, the boxes represent entities, and the linking lines represent relationships. One variation on the node-link diagram is the organization chart.

Example: If A and B should work together on a project, who in the organization should be involved in setting this up. *[Query, trace upward paths from both A and B noting all the boxes and the individuals these boxes represent].*

Node link diagrams (second example): Show network links between computers. Different styles of lines represent different rates of data communication.

Example: Can the network function when a node fails? *[Query, node X is the sole link connecting any pair of components].*

Example: Is data bandwidth adequate between nodes? *[Query, locate end points and trace paths between them, line style shows the capacity of links.]*

of interconnected pattern-processing modules. Input patterns from the visual world activate patterns of responding, such as sequences of eye movements. Visual thinking also involves the interplay between patterns of activity in the nonvisual verbal-processing centers of the brain.

Although pattern finding is something that everyone can do because it is a fundamental part of the process of seeing, designers must have an additional skill. They must have the metacognitive skill of seeing critically. This is very different from simply seeing that a pattern is present and using that pattern for some cognitive task like finding a route using a map. The map designer must critically analyze which combinations of patterns will provide the best support for the set of cognitive tasks a map supports.

Critical seeing involves understanding the visual tasks that will be undertaken by a viewer of a graphic and predicting how easily they can be performed with alternative designs. This ability may seem intuitive to the skilled designer, but this intuition is hard-won through years of experience honing critical perception. Because pattern perception is so central, we will return to this and many of the other issues raised in this chapter.

Chapter 4

Color

Most large animals have worse color vision than humans. Color vision is of little benefit to grass eaters like zebras and cows—these animals have only two dimensions of color vision. The motion of a tiger's prey is more critical than its color, and although cats, like grazing animals, have the physiological basis for two dimensions of color, it is extremely difficult to train them to respond to color. For the most part, they behave as if they

Color vision makes it much easier to see the fruit of the West African Akee Tree.

Visual Thinking for Information Design. DOI: https://doi.org/10.1016/B978-0-12-823567-6.00004-5

66

live in a gray-scale world. On the other hand, color is invaluable to fruit eaters; color lets them see the oranges in the tree or the red berries in the bush. Birds have even better color vision than humans, being able to distinguish four or more dimensions. Humans and the other great apes, omnivorous hunter-gatherers that we are, have three dimensions of color.

The purpose of this chapter is to develop a theory-based approach to how color should be used in design. This will be somewhat incomplete because color is a complex technical subject, although a surprisingly small amount of theory is needed to derive the most important aesthetic principles. The parts of color theory not covered include colorimetry and color reproduction. Colorimetry is the discipline dealing with the precise measurement and specification of color.* Color reproduction is the discipline dealing with how colors are printed on paper, as well as methods for transforming colors from some display medium, such as a computer monitor, to another, such as printed paper through color gamut mapping.*

THE COLOR-PROCESSING MACHINERY

There are two basic types of light receptors in the retina at the back of the eyeball: rods and cones. Rods, the most numerous type, are specialized for very low light levels. Rods are wasted on modern humans because they are overloaded at the light levels of our artificially lit world. These days most people rarely try to get around under starlight, and this is no longer an important survival skill. Unfortunately, we have no way of trading our rod receptors for cone receptors.

Cone receptors are the basis for normal daytime vision, and they come in three subtypes—short-wavelength sensitive, middle-wavelength sensitive, and long-wavelength sensitive. These three different types of cones mean color vision is fundamentally three-dimensional. This is the reason that televisions and monitors have three types of liquid crystal filters, or three different-colored light-emitting phosphors in older cathode-ray tube monitors.

David Williams, at the University of Rochester, has recently succeeded in obtaining images of the human retina and classifying the cones. Here are examples from two different people.

What is immediately apparent in these images of retinas is that there are far fewer short-wavelength-sensitive cones (blue) than middle-or long-wavelength-sensitive cones. Compounding this, the few short-wavelength-sensitive cones are less sensitive to light than either the middle- or long-wavelength-sensitive cones.

*The classic text dealing with color measurement as well as basic results is G. Wyszecki and W.S. Styles, 1982. *Color Science: Concepts and Methods, Quantitative Data and Formulae* (2nd ed.). John Wiley & Sons, Inc., New York. As of 2007, it is still in press. Charles Poynton's site http://www.poynton.com/ColorFAQ.html is a very useful source of technical color information.

*See M. Stone. 2003. *A Field Guide to Digital Color*. A.K. Peters. The effects of mixing paints and printing inks are complex because of the ways light interacts with pigments—mixing colored lights is much simpler. Still, a reasonably complete range of colors can be produced with the colors cyan, magenta, and yellow. The reason these are different than the red, green, and blue of monitors is that these printing dyes subtract light reflected by underlying white paper, as opposed to emitting it.

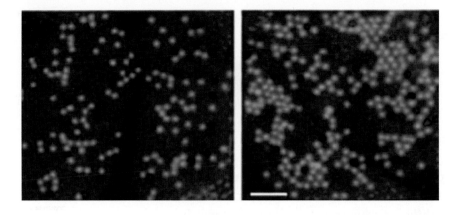

Cones in the fovea where there are no rods. Those sensitive to short, medium, and long wavelengths are colored blue, green, and red, respectively.

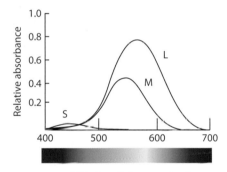

Sensitivity functions for the three classes of cone receptor. Cone receptors are sensitive to light having wavelengths between 400 and 700 nanometers (1 nm = 10^{-9} meters).

Note that the sensitivity distributions of long (L)– and medium (M)–wavelength-sensitive cones overlap considerably. The brain takes the difference between the two signals to get useful hue information.

It is impossible to reproduce pure spectral colors with printing inks so the color bands below should only be taken as rough approximations to the actual hues.

A consequence of our having few and weak blue-sensitive cones is that it is a mistake to show text or anything else with detail using blue on a dark background. The result is usually illegible.

Showing small blue text on a black
background is a bad idea.
There is insufficient luminance contrast.

A related problem occurs when using yellow for text. A pure yellow hue excites both the numerous middle- and long-wavelength cones, making yellow the lightest of all pure hues. Yellow can be almost as light as white, and small yellow text on a white background is extremely hard to read, but pure yellow is very distinct on a black background.

Showing small yellow text on a white
background is a bad idea.
There is insufficient luminance contrast.

Showing small yellow text on a white
background is a bad idea.
There is insufficient luminance contrast.

Another interesting feature of the images of retinas on the previous page is the way the red- and green-colored cones are clumped together. We can see considerable detail in black and white images because for black-white detail it is only necessary for black and white parts of the image to fall on two or more different cone receptors, no matter which type. But the patchy nature of the different cone types means that we are far less able to see detail where the differences are purely chromatic.

OPPONENT PROCESS THEORY

A major transformation in the color signal from the receptors occurs in the area V1, where information traveling along the optic nerve first arrives at the cortex. Neural networks add and subtract the cone signals in different ways, transforming them into what are called the *color-opponent channels.* There are three channels, designated *red-green*, *yellow-blue*, and *black-white* (or luminance), respectively. The red-green channel represents the *difference* between the signal from the middle- and long-wavelength-sensitive cones.

This allows us to be highly sensitive to subtle red-green contrasts despite the overlap in the cone-sensitivity functions. The luminance channel *combines* the outputs of long- and middle-wavelength-sensitive cones. The yellow-blue channel represents the *difference* between the luminance

*Color opponent theory can be traced back to Ewald Hering who published his ideas in Vienna in 1878.

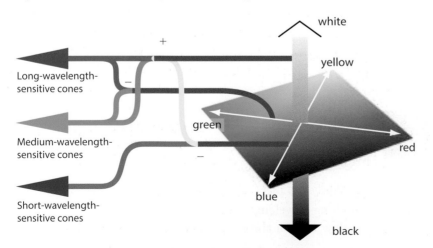

In V1, the raw signals from the cones in the retina are transformed. Some neurons compute differences between red- and green-sensitive cone signals. Some neurons compute the sum of red- and green-sensitive cones. Still others compute yellow-blue differences.

The result is three kinds of color signals that are called color-opponent channels.

The reality is actually more complex, but opponent channel theory is an extremely useful simplification.

channel and the blue cone signals. Note that although the black-white channel combines two types of cone information, it also differentiates in a spatial sense. Black-white differences are calculated simultaneously between all adjacent regions in the retina.

CHANNEL PROPERTIES

Most of the important principles for effectively using color in design can be derived from an understanding of the red-green, yellow-blue, and black-white color channels. What follows is a kind of annotated list of channel properties.

Contrast: A phenomenon known as simultaneous contrast occurs in each of the channels. The effect of simultaneous contrast is distortion of the appearance of a patch of color in a way that increases the difference between a color and its surroundings. This is called lightness or brightness contrast when it occurs in the black-white channel and chromatic contrast when it occurs in either the red-green or yellow-blue channel.

The two gray bars are exactly the same shade, but because of simultaneous lightness contrast the bar on the left seems darker than the one on the right.

Although contrast is often thought of as an *illusion*, a kind of visual error, the mechanisms of contrast help us see surface colors in the real world. Contrast comes about because the visual system is better at determining the *differences* between patches of light in the world than how much light is present as it might be measured by a light meter. Difference information helps us discount the amount of light in our environment, enabling us to perceive how light or dark the surfaces of objects are whether they are seen on a dull winter day or a bright sunny day at the beach. It is because the brain is sensitive to differences and not absolute values that we can reproduce a reasonable facsimile of a beach scene at the movie theatre, despite the fact that there may be one-hundredth the amount of light reflecting from the screen, compared to the real-world scene.

Chromatic contrast occurs in the red-green and yellow-blue channels. Its effects are much more complex and harder to predict than gray-scale contrast.

The two yellowish bars have the same hue, but because of simultaneous chromatic contrast the one on the left seems more yellow and the one on the right, greener.

Unique hues: The opponent process theory suggests that the colors black, white, red, green, yellow, and blue are special. Each occurs when there is a strong signal (either positive or negative) on one of the channels and a neutral signal on the other two channels. Confirming their importance, a remarkable study of more than one hundred human languages by Brent Berlin and Paul Kay carried out in the 1960s showed these basic color terms are the most commonly used no matter what the language.[*]

[*]B. Berlin and P. Kay. 1969. *Basic Color Terms: Their Universality and Evolution*. University of California Press, Berkeley.

Sensitivity to spatial detail: The luminance channel has much greater capacity to convey detailed information than the chromatic channels. The patterns below show that we can still see large shapes represented chromatically, but the fine pattern is much harder to see expressed through chromatic differences than when expressed through black-white differences.

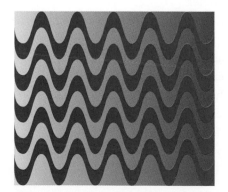 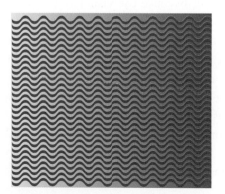 

Motion: The luminance channel can convey motion information much more effectively than the chromatic cannels. When moving shapes are shown in red and green only, their motion appears to slow down.

Stereoscopic depth: This is the kind of depth information we get from having two eyes. The brain's processing of stereoscopic depth information is done via the luminance channel.

Shape-from-shading: We understand the shape of three-dimensional surfaces from the pattern of shading that comes from the way different facets of a surface are oriented to the light. The luminance channel can process shape-from-shading, whereas the chromatic channels cannot. In the illustration below, a black and white photograph of a shaded surface has been doctored so that the black-white sequence has been transformed into a red-green sequence. In this way, the original image that stimulated only the luminance channel has been modified so that it only stimulates the red-green channel. Although sharp boundaries are still clear, the topography of the shape has become virtually meaningless.

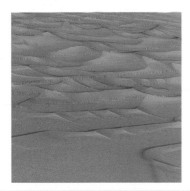

This image has had all of its gray-scale values transformed into red-green values. Because shape-from-shading processing is based on luminance channel information it is difficult to interpret.

This is a NASA image of sand dunes on Mars taken by the Viking Lander. Note how readily we see the different gray values as making up a 3D undulating surface.

Saturation: The more vivid a color, the more saturated it is said to be. More saturated colors are those that have strong signals on one or both of the red-green and yellow-blue chromatic channels.

Low saturation   High saturation   Low saturation   High saturation

Maximum saturation varies with luminance: When colors are dark there is a smaller difference signal on the chromatic channels, and saturations are lower for dark colors. When colors are light there is also usually a reduction in saturation for reasons having to do with color reproduction technology rather than perception. Colors on a computer monitor are limited by the maximum amount of light coming from the red, green, and blue pixels. The lightest (or brightest) color is necessarily white because this occurs when all the pixels are fully on. The next lightest colors are low-saturation pastel hues. A similar effect occurs for printing inks.

Color assimilation: Under certain circumstances color patches do not contrast with adjacent colors, rather they take on some of their hue. In other words, rather than increasing in color difference, the perceived difference between colors is decreased. This is called *assimilation*. In the example below, the arcs to the left and right have the same colors, but they seem very different. The circumstances under which it occurs are poorly understood but involve a complex interplay of pattern and color.

Luminance, lightness, brightness: *Luminance* refers to the physical amount of light as it might be measured by an instrument such as a photometer. The term *lightness* is used when discussing surface colors, and *brightness* is generally used when discussing emitted light. Both terms, however, apply to the amount of light coming from a particular part of the visual field and therefore to signals that affect the luminance channel.

Luminance nonlinearity: The luminance channel is nonlinear. We are more sensitive to dark gray differences than to light differences, although this effect also depends on the background. On top of this, the background is important. With a dark gray background, our sensitivity is increased to gray differences in the midrange. With a light background, our sensitivity is increased to differences near white. This effect is sometimes called *sharpening*.

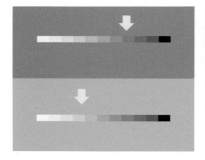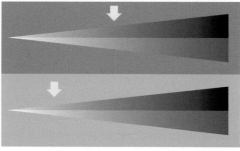

The top and bottom inner patterns are the same. Only the background is different.

Arrows show the points where sharpening occurs.

Color segmentation: The visual system has a strong tendency to segment smoothly changing colors into regions consisting of the unique hues.

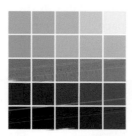

Notice how the eye tends to divide the smoothly varying colors in the square on the left into regions of red, green, yellow, and blue. To a lesser extent, purple and orange can be seen. It is almost impossible to see the neutral gray in the center. In the segmented version (on the right), more colors are clearly evident even though there are actually fewer present.

Color blindness: People who are color blind (about 8 percent of males) are missing the red-green channel, and therefore have a two-dimensional rather than a three-dimensional color space. They can still distinguish colors that differ in the yellow-blue direction, and their ability to see gray-scale is unaffected. Yellow-blue color blindness is much less common.

Color-blind individuals will have difficulty distinguishing the patch of green colors from the surrounding red colors.

They will have no difficulty distinguishing a patch of yellow colors from the surrounding blue colors.

Chromatic color as a property of surfaces: A major function of visual processing is to let us perceive the properties of surfaces in the environment, rather than the amount of light coming from those surfaces. Many of the mechanisms of color vision exist to support this function. Adaptation in the receptors means that we are relatively insensitive to overall changes in light levels. Contrast mechanisms make us more sensitive to local changes in surface colors, rather than differences in light and shade across a scene.

Color and attention: As discussed in Chapter 2, the pattern-finding mechanisms of the brain can be tuned for color. This allows for rapid visual searches for things that are of particular colors. But color search also depends on how many other colors there are in the environment. If all the world is gray, a patch of vivid color pops out. If the world is a riot of colors then a visual search for a particular hue becomes difficult.

Color solids: The three-dimensional nature of color space is a straightforward consequence of having three cone types in the retina. But if we wish to view this three-dimensional space, how exactly should the colors be laid out? Here are just two of the many possible solutions.

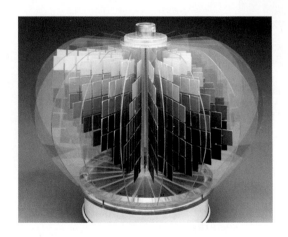

This is a set of calibrated color samples. Each is designed to be equally different from the adjacent sample making it an example of a *uniform color space*.

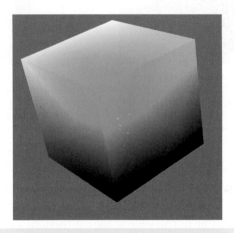

This is the outside of the cube of colors that can be represented on a computer monitor by combinations of the outputs of the red, green, and blue guns. The space is not perceptually uniform.

Color appearance: It only takes a combination of three lights (red, green, and blue) to create a full range of colors (for example, a photographic image reproduced on a computer monitor), and this is why color vision is said to be three-dimensional. Nevertheless, color *appearance* has more than three dimensions. The reason is spatial. A patch of color is never seen in isolation, and its appearance is affected by the colors that surround it, its orientation with respect to the light source, whether it is perceived as lying in or out of shadow, the texture of the surface on which it lies, and so on. Colors like brown and olive green only occur through contrast with surrounding colors. A color patch that seems brown when viewed on a white background will be perceived as orange when viewed in isolation in a dark room.

This remarkable demonstration by R. Beau Lotto of University College, London, shows how dramatically our perception of light and shade can affect our perception of color. The (apparently) brown square at the top center has exactly the same color as the (apparently) yellow square in the center of the front face. If you do not believe it, cut a small hole in a piece of white paper and use it to examine each patch of color with the surroundings blocked out.

PRINCIPLES FOR DESIGN

The remainder of this chapter is devoted to applying color theory in elaborating a set of principles for the use of color in design. The approach is utilitarian, emphasizing clarity and support for visual tasks, but should not prevent designers from creating graphics that are visually delightful. There is a huge scope for creativity within the functional framework developed here.

SHOWING DETAIL

The most important single principle in the use of color is that whenever detailed information is to be shown, luminance contrast is necessary. Of course, black and white give the most extreme contrast possible. However, it is also possible to get excellent luminance contrast with yellow on black or dark blue on white. As graphical features get larger, so the need for extreme luminance contrast declines.

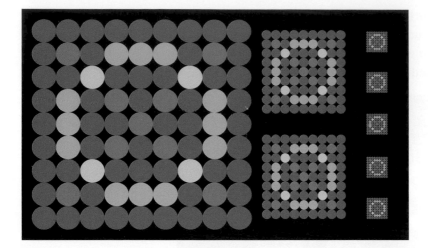

In the larger version of this pattern, the colors are the most salient features. In the much smaller versions to the right, the luminance values dominate so that a circular 0 pattern becomes the most distinct feature.

Luminance contrast is especially critical for small text. The International Standards Organization (ISO) recommends a ratio of at least 3:1 between the luminance of text and the luminance of the background. This severely restricts the range of colors that can be used for text. We can have black (or very dark-colored text) on a background that is white, or consists of light pastel hues—or we can have the reverse. When design elements are very large, for example in a poster title, luminance contrast is less critical and design can be given free rein. The red-green and yellow-blue channels do not convey fine detail, but they are just as effective as black and white for making large patterns distinct.

APRIL is the cruellest month, breeding
Lilacs out of the dead land, mixing
Memory and desire, stirring
Dull roots with spring rain.
Winter kept us warm, covering
Earth in forgetful snow, feeding
A little life with dried tubers.

T.S. Eliot

APRIL is the cruellest month, breeding
Lilacs out of the dead land, mixing
Memory and desire, stirring
Dull roots with spring rain.
Winter kept us warm, covering
Earth in forgetful snow, feeding
A little life with dried tubers.

T.S. Eliot

APRIL

When text is small, it is essential that there be luminance contrast with the background color. Notice how the text is hardest to read when the luminance contrast is lowest. When text is big, anything goes.

COLOR-CODING INFORMATION

Perhaps the most important use of color is to indicate categories of information. In this land-use map, color codes are used to show different land-use zones.

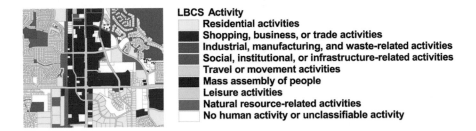

LBCS Activity
Residential activities
Shopping, business, or trade activities
Industrial, manufacturing, and waste-related activities
Social, institutional, or infrastructure-related activities
Travel or movement activities
Mass assembly of people
Leisure activities
Natural resource-related activities
No human activity or unclassifiable activity

In the design of color codes, the two primary considerations must be *visual distinctness*, to support visual search operations, and *learnability*, so that particular colors come to "stand for" particular entities. When learnability is the issue, it is important to use the unique hues first—red, green, yellow, and blue—followed by other colors that have relatively consistent names—pink, brown, orange, gray, and purple.♦

♦Although there may be quite large individual differences in how people perceive colors, when it comes to labeling them with words we appear to have a shared system.

S.B.K.A. Jameson, N. Alvarado, and M.K. Szeszel. 2005. Semantic and perceptual representations of color: Evidence for a shared color naming function. *The Journal of Cognition and Culture.* 5(3–4): 427–486.

There are strict limits as to how many colors can be used effectively as codes. If a design is complex and the symbols are quite small, then no more than a dozen codes can be used with complete reliability.♦ The main reason why we cannot use more colors is that the backgrounds can distort the appearance of a small patch of symbol color leading to the confusion of one symbol with another.

♦There are many studies designed to answer the question "How many colors can be used reliably in a symbol set?" yielding a range of answers, depending on exactly how they were conducted. But the number of colors recommended is always between six and twelve.

To effectively support *visual search* the colors of the background and the other symbols in the set are as important as the symbol being searched. When we conduct a visual search for an object having a particular color, our brains tune our visual systems so that neurons sensitive to that hue get to "shout louder" than neurons tuned to other colors. There are, however, limits to this capability. A strong pop-out effect depends both on the other colored objects in the scene and on the background color.

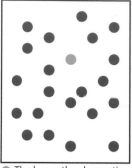 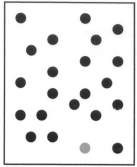 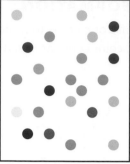

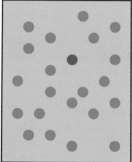 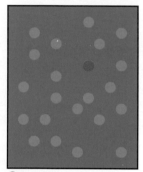 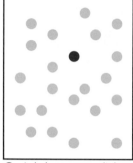

● The larger the chromatic difference between the target symbol and the other symbols, the easier the search.

● When there is only a small color difference from non–target symbols, the search is difficult.

● When there are many non–target symbol colors, the search is the most difficult.

● If non–target symbols are similar to the background, they are easy to exclude from the visual search.

● A luminance difference plus a chromatic difference from other symbols and the background leads to the easiest search.

● A dark target on a light background with light non–target symbols can be as effective as the reverse.

LARGE AND SMALL AREAS

More complex designs often include color-coded background regions as well as color-coded symbols. Because of different channel properties, small areas should be strongly colored and have black-white channel contrast with larger background areas if they are to be distinct. Large areas can have more subdued colors.

When small symbols must be displayed against a colored background, it can be difficult to come up with a set of colors that are both distinct from each other and from the background. Using low-saturation colors for large areas generally makes the task easier. Because we are far more sensitive to color differences between larger areas, strongly saturated colors are unnecessary for large objects or backgrounds. Also, color contrast will distort the perceived color of small symbols less if the background colors are low in saturation.

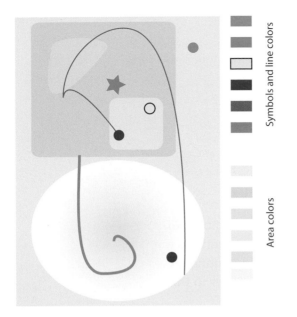

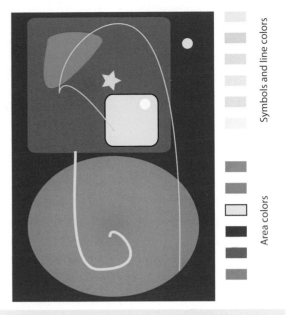

GOOD. This example uses high saturation (strong colors) to code small areas such as symbols and lines. Larger background areas are all light and low saturation.

A black contrasting border is used to separate the yellow circle from its background because both have similar luminance.

BAD. This example shows what happens when the colors used for small areas and large areas are switched. The color codes used for the symbols and lines are difficult to discriminate because of contrast effects.

Besides being completely ineffective, the second example would generally be regarded as unattractive.

EMPHASIS AND HIGHLIGHTING

A strong signal on any of the opponent channels will attract attention better than a weak signal. Also, the strength of the signal depends on the difference between a visual object and its background. Objects that have reduced contrast with their backgrounds are naturally less salient.

Liberty consists in the freedom to do everything which injures no one else;
hence the exercise of the natural rights of each man has no limits except those
which assure to the other members of the society the enjoyment of the same rights.
These limits can only be determined by law.

Law can only prohibit such actions as are hurtful to society.
Nothing may be prevented which is not forbidden by law,
and no one may be forced to do anything not provided for by law.

Declaration of the Rights of Man
National Assembly of France 1989

A common mistake, often seen in PowerPoint slides, is to highlight something using color in such a way that luminance contrast is reduced. The highlighted text shown above is *less* distinct than the other text even though it uses a saturated hue.

Liberty consists in the freedom to do everything which *injures no one else;* hence the exercise of the natural rights of each man has no limits except those which assure to the other members of the society the enjoyment of the same rights. These limits can only be determined by law.

Law can only prohibit *such actions as are hurtful to society.* Nothing may be prevented which is not forbidden by law, and no one may be forced to do anything not provided for by law.

Declaration of the Rights of Man
National Assembly of France 1989

It is often more effective to emphasize text by reducing the contrast of the other text, but care must be taken to maintain sufficient luminance contrast for clarity. Of course, text can also be highlighted by tinting the background, not the letters themselves, as has been shown earlier in this chapter.

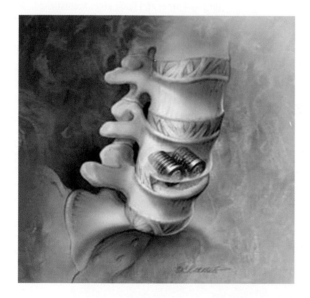

This illustration of a lumbar spinal fusion technique, by medical illustrator Christy Crames, has highlighted the critical area of interest by de-emphasizing the background through the use of neutral tones with some low-saturation blues. The critical area of interest is rendered in higher contrast and with the color red appearing only in this area.

Color highlighting is most effective for visual search when only a few colors are involved. The fewer the colors, the faster they can be found.

Highlighting in images can be done using similar principles. Increasing the color saturation of an area of interest and decreasing the saturation of everything else is a useful method. Other methods include darkening, or lightening everything not of interest, or blurring it.

Color is most effective as a highlighter when there is only a single color used, other than black and white.

COLOR SEQUENCES

A particular specialized use of color is the color-coding of maps. A map need not be geographical; we might have a map of the stock market, a map of radiation levels in the cosmos, or generally speaking, of any quantity that varies over a plane. Some maps have well-established color sequences already defined by convention. Usually in these cases it is unnecessary and unwise to promote an alternative. An example is the convention used by geographers to show the height of land with a color sequence that starts with green for the land transitions through light and dark brown in the mountains and often ends with white at the peaks.

There are two primary tasks supported by color sequences used with maps. First, it allows people to perceive the spatial layout of *patterns in the data*, such as the shape and location of the hills, ridges, and valleys. Second, we can read *quantitative values* from the map; for example, judging the height or energy level at a particular location.

Because shape perception is based mainly on luminance channel information, color sequences (called *colormaps*) that vary mainly in luminance will be the most effective in revealing patterns in the data. But there is a drawback to using a simple gray sequence.• Contrast effects in gray-scale sequence can lead to very large errors when it comes to reading off data values using a key. The best solution may often be to provide a sequence that spirals up through color space, starting off with a dark color and selecting a series of colors, each of which has higher luminance than the previous one.

•In a study published in 1988, I measured errors as large as 20% of the data range for gray-sequence colormaps.

C. Ware. 1988. Color sequences for univariate maps: Theory, experiments and principles. *IEEE Computer Graphics and Applications*. Sept. 41–49.

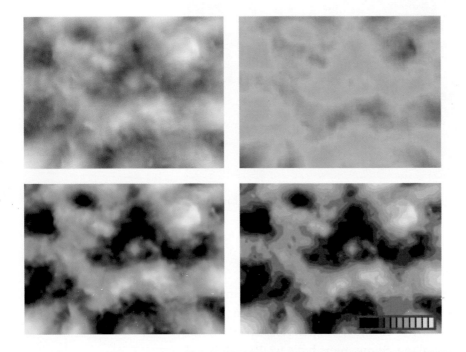

The data shown is the height of the ocean in the Western Pacific Ocean in the region of the Kiroshio current. On the upper left is a simple gray scale. It is clear and unambiguous with respect to lows and highs. The green-red colormap is poor, because of the low resolution of the red-green channel. The rainbow colormap on the lower left can be confusing and emphasizes certain features while failing to show others. The double ended colormap on the lower right from Francesca Samsel reveals the most detail, because it goes from dark blue to white to a dark reddish brown, effectively doubling the luminance range.

Zero is often an important number in data analysis, and sometimes a color sequence is needed that represents zero in an intuitive way. A good method for showing zero is to use a neutral value on the red-green and yellow-blue channels. Increasingly saturated values can be used to represent values above and below zero.

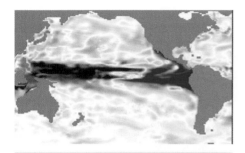

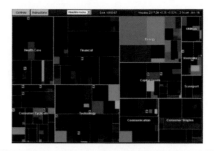

This map shows temperature differences (from normal) for the Pacific Ocean at 100 meters depth during an El Niño period. Warmer than usual is shown as red. Cooler than usual is shown as blue. Zero difference is shown as white.

This map of the stock market uses color coding to show how different sectors of the stock market have gone up or down. Increasing values are shown in green. Decreasing values are shown in red. Zero change is shown in black.

One kind of colormap often used by scientists is an approximation to the spectrum of light (purple-blue-cyan-green-yellow-red). Because this represents a sequence of wavelengths of light, it is often erroneously presumed to be a perceptual sequence. A simple experiment will show this not to be the case. Give a number of people a set of color chips consisting of red, green, yellow, and blue. Ask them to put them in a sequence. You will get many orderings, and the spectrum sequence is no more likely than any other. However, if you give them more chips, they may come up with a circle arrangement because each small section of the spectrum has a perceptual ordering. For comparison, ask those same people to order a set of gray chips ranging from black to white. The result will always be either a black-to-white ordering or a white-to-black ordering. Parts of the spectrum are perceptually ordered, but the whole spectrum is not. The spectrum may be useful for reading values from data using a color key and this makes it a good choice for a weather map, but it will not be the best for revealing patterns.

COLOR ON SHADED SURFACES

What does it take to see both the shape of a shaded surface and the colored patterns that are painted on that surface? Shape from shading information is conveyed by the luminance channel, and any colored pattern that interferes with luminance channel information destroys our ability to see the shape of the surface.

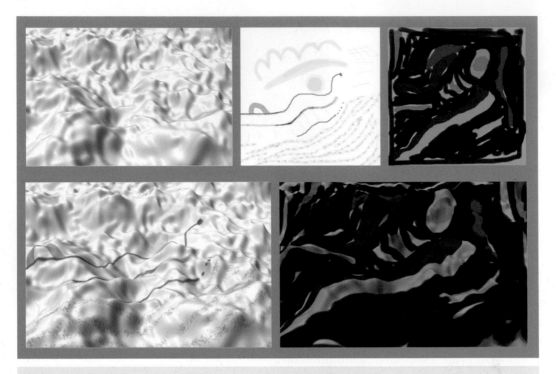

Adding the light-colored pattern (top center) to a shaded surface (top left) interferes little with our perception of surface shape as the combined image (lower left) shows. Adding a dark-colored pattern with strongly saturated colors (top right) to the same shaded surface almost completely destroys our ability to see the surface shape (lower right).

SEMANTICS OF COLOR

Colors are often used symbolically. In western culture, red represents danger, heat, and stop; green represents go, safety, and renewal; blue represents cold; white represents purity; and so on. Some of these meanings are well entrenched. Changing stop signs to the color green would have disastrous consequences. Such color meanings are culturally determined, and so a particular choice of colors may have a different meaning in another country. For example, in China red is used to symbolize good fortune and renewal. In most of Asia, white is the color for mourning, whereas in the west it is black. Designers for international markets must take such color symbolisms into account.

Other semantic mappings relating to quantity may be more universal. Quantities that are larger should generally be mapped to colors that are more distinct. This visually means that more saturated colors should be used to represent greater quantity. Similarly, darker colors on a light background or lighter colors on a dark background can be used to indicate greater quantity.

Six different ways of showing greater quantity. All involve increasing the relative difference from the background color.

For all but the simplest designs, the choice of a set of colors is a complex problem that typically involves tradeoffs. Every piece of information cannot be maximally distinct. Considerations such as the consistency of design across multiple graphics used in a document or a website may also restrict design options. As a rule of thumb, the most common and most important visual queries should be given the most weight. This means that the most distinctive hues should be reserved for the most commonly accessed symbols and patterns in a design.

CONCLUSION

The essence of color opponent theory is simple. The image on the retina is transformed in the visual cortex; the value at every point is transformed into red-green, yellow-blue, and black-white difference signals. Also larger regions of an image are evaluated with respect to its adjoining regions in terms of how much they differ in each of the channels. The luminance channel is capable of conveying far more spatial detail than either of the chromatic channels.

Much of the functional aesthetics of color can be derived from this theory. One consequence of this is that colors are changed in appearance by adjacent colors. This is called simultaneous lightness or chromatic contrast. As a result, we can reliably use only a handful of very different colors symbolically to label information. If we try to use more, contrast effects mean that colors will be confused. Also, contrast effects mean that the appearance of a specific hue can only be judged in the context of a particular set of surrounding colors. Not only that, but color appearance depends on the amount of area covered by each patch of color; large areas change the color appearance of small areas, much more than small areas change the appearance of large areas. Because of this it is generally better if large areas have subdued colors. Also, to make small areas distinct they should be strongly colored to counter the lack of spatial resolution in the red-green and yellow-blue channels.

Another consequence of opponent-channel theory is that red, green, yellow, blue, black, and white are special. They each produce the most extreme signal on one channel while being neutral with respect to the other channels. These are the most distinct and easily identified colors and form the ideal labels, all other considerations being equal.

Only the black-white channel is capable of conveying much detail and so dark-light contrast is *essential* if detail is to be shown. This is true for text, fine lines, and fine textures. The black-white channel is also essential to show the shape of curved surfaces through shading, and this means that smooth graduations of darkness and lightness will be perceived largely as shading differences.

Unlike gray-scale gradients, smooth graduations of color tend to be perceptually categorized into regions of red, yellow, green, and blue. If it is necessary to present a hue so that it can be properly judged, it is useful to isolate it with a neutral black, white, or gray border. Even better is to see it in context. Computer graphics allows this; the color of a graphical object can be adjusted *in situ* in a developing design.

We have just listed the main properties needed to make design decisions leading to visual clarity. Not surprisingly, there is a lot more to the use of color than this. Color design is subtle and can be a source of beauty and pleasure or disgust and irritation. Mostly this is a matter of socially constructed taste—there are no absolute standards. Our goal in this book is to find the bedrock of functional aesthetics in the wiring of the brain, and sadly, we have little to say about beauty.

Chapter 5

Getting the Information: Visual Space and Time

"It is one thing to say with the psalmist 'I lift mine eyes up to the hills'—it is another thing to drag one's carcass up there."

GK Chesterton, paraphrased by John Prange

Moving our eyes is the lowest-cost method we have for getting additional information about our environment. It has such a low cognitive cost that we are not even aware that we are making eye movements several times a second. In visual data searches "drag[ing] one's carcass up there" is what we do when we search through a jumbled filing cabinet to find information, often entirely losing our train of thought in the process. It is also what we do when we travel a thousand miles to an information-sharing meeting.

Often when we engage in business travel, our goal is to meet people and discuss a project or gain access to concentrated information, for example,

Visual Thinking for Information Design. DOI: https://doi.org/10.1016/B978-0-12-823567-6.00005-7

at a conference. These are essentially cognitive activities, and so the cost of travel can be thought of as a cognitive cost. From a business perspective, even the social alliances that are formed are communication channels for the flow of valuable information and ideas. Although sound can be transmitted cheaply, sincerity, or the lack of it, is conveyed by subtle facial expressions, which is why face-to-face meetings are often worth the cost of travel. During the covid-19 epidemic the risks of travel dramatically increased and video-coferencing was widely adopted, not because of a reduction in value for in-person meetings but because they came at a higher cost.

Eye movements, rummaging through filing cabinets, and business travel are ultimately all methods for traversing space to get information into our working memory systems, though they differ enormously in efficiency. It is in this light that we consider the structure of three-dimensional space.

This map of the region around Cambridge, England, shows the times to reach various regions by means of public transportation.

Some outlying villages can be reached as quickly as places on the outskirts of the city. Others are inaccessible. If the reason for travel were to obtain information, these times should be regarded as cognitive costs.

The colors give the travel times in hours.

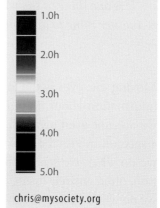

chris@mysociety.org

With technology we can radically change the costs of access, storage, and transmission for both visual and auditory information. For example, *high-quality* video conferencing systems can provide all of the visual and sound cues for the social dynamics of meetings to be preserved. The result can be substantial cost savings from reduced air travel, and meeting expenses, as well as greater overall productivity since more time can be spent in environments conducive to cognitive work.

High-quality video conferencing systems can transmit many of the social cues that make face-to-face meetings important.

Conversely, low-quality video conferencing systems fail to convey the subtle cues of expression and gesture important for judging intentions.

This chapter is about the perceptual and cognitive structure of space, taking into account both how depth is perceived and the costs of navigation to access information. We begin with an introduction of the theory of depth perception.

DEPTH PERCEPTION AND CUE THEORY

It seems incontestable to say that we live in a three-dimensional world. But "live in" is a weasel phrase. The *physical* world is indeed three-dimensional, for most practical purposes. Although some theoretical physicists believe that all matter is constructed of strings in twelve-dimensional space, this only matters at a subatomic scale. The cognitive organism, however, acts on visual information that is imaged on the retina. This leads to perceived space having dimensions that are very different from the spaces mathematicians and physicists consider because each dimension has different affordances. The perceptual *egocentric* space is commonly thought of in terms of the *up* dimension, the *sideways* dimension, and the *towards-away* dimension.

In Chapter 3, we considered visual pattern processing that occurs on information captured by the *up* and *sideways* dimensions. Now we turn our attention to the information available to the eye and brain from the towards-away dimension. This information is contained in what psychologists call *depth cues*. Most depth cues consist of environmental information that we use to judge distances from our particular viewpoint. There is much less information available in the *towards-away* directions than *up* and *sideways* directions, since the latter is directly available from the image on the retina. This is why perception is sometimes called a 2.5-dimensional phenomenon with the 0.5 referring to the *towards-away* information. The 0.5 should not be taken literally; *towards-away* information is much less than a half of what is provided by the other dimensions because we cannot see through most objects and so for every one of the million brain pixels recording up and sideways information there is only, at best, one point of depth information.

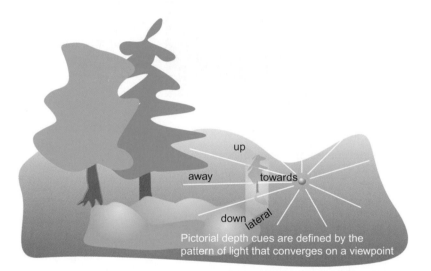

Pictorial depth cues are defined by the pattern of light that converges on a viewpoint

Some of the depth cues are called pictorial because they can be used in static pictures.

One way of thinking about pictorial cues is in terms of a pane of glass which we look through with one eye holding steady at a particular viewpoint. If we were to put dabs of paint on the glass pane, corresponding to the colors in the world behind it, we would capture all of the pictorial depth cues because pictorial cues are defined by the projection of points in space onto a plane.

Depth cues can be divided into those that are *pictorial*, and those that are *nonpictorial*. Pictorial depth cues can be reproduced in a photograph or a realistic painting. First and most powerful among these is occlusion objects that visually block other objects appear closer. There is a whole set of pictorial depth cues that derives from the geometry of perspective including size gradients, texture gradients, and linear perspective. Other pictorial depth cues are cast shadows, height on the picture plane, shape from shading, depth of focus, size relative to known objects, and atmospheric contrast reduction. The nonpictorial depth cues are stereopsis (arising from our having two eyes), structure from motion (which we get as we move through the world), as well as lesser effects like focusing of the lens in the eye, and the convergence of the two eyes that occurs when we fixate near objects.

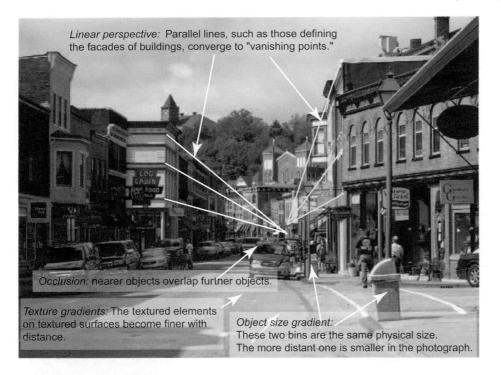

Linear perspective: Parallel lines, such as those defining the facades of buildings, converge to "vanishing points."

Occlusion: nearer objects overlap further objects.

Texture gradients: The textured elements on textured surfaces become finer with distance.

Object size gradient: These two bins are the same physical size. The more distant one is smaller in the photograph.

Pictorial depth cues do not have to be applied as a complete package in an all-or-nothing fashion; they can be applied independently according to the goals of the design. This means that the choice of the designer is not three-dimensional versus two-dimensional, but which of the depth cues to apply. Each of them has unique properties that can support different kinds of visual queries.

Occlusion: Objects near to us block or visually *occlude* objects further away. An object that occludes another appears closer. Occlusion is the strongest depth cue, and if it is placed in competition with another, such as size constancy, occlusion wins.

Occlusion provides both a method and a metaphor for rank-ordering information with the most important partially occluding the less important. When designing with occlusion it is critical that the partially occluded objects can still be identified. Interactive computer applications allow for occluded information to be brought to the front with a mouse click.

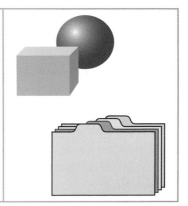

Perspective: *Size gradients:* More distant objects are smaller on the picture plane than similarly sized nearby objects.

Size changes can be used to provide a visual metaphor for the relative importance of different information objects. Using this cue has the advantage that less important information takes up less space than more important information.

Perspective: *Texture gradients:* There is a reduction in size and increase in density of texture elements with distance. The texture elements on a ground plane provide a size reference for objects, although most textures provide less support than a grid in making size judgments. Unfortunately, fine textures are usually not reproduced on computer displays, which can be a major shortcoming.

Linear perspective: Projections of parallel lines converge on the picture plane. A grid of lines is a common device used in scientific illustrations to provide a reference plane for judging the three-dimensional layout of objects. A grid also provides a ubiquitous ruler for visual queries aimed at judging the sizes of objects.

R.B. Wilhelmson, et al. 1990. A study of the evolution of a numerically modeled severe storm. *International Journal of Supercomputing Applications*. 4: 20-36.

Cast shadows: The shadow cast by one object on another provides information about the distance between them. The height of the two cyan balls above the checkerboard can be seen from the shadows. The actual depth information in this image is provided by the checkered ground plane. The depth of the balls is perceptually inferred from its relationship to the perspective grid.

The magenta balls, having no shadows, have nothing to tie them to the ground plane; they seem to float at an indeterminate distance.

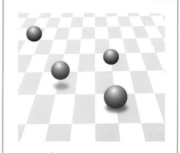

Height on picture plane: Because our visual world is dominated by the ground plane, objects higher up in the visual field are generally further away. Placing an object higher up on a picture plane can be used to represent greater distance.

This simple method is often used in nonperspective maps to indicate relative distance from a certain point, typically at the bottom of the map. (Note that sometimes this is called a *parallel* or *axonometric projection*.)

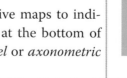

Shading: The surfaces of objects reflect more or less light depending on how they are oriented toward the light source.

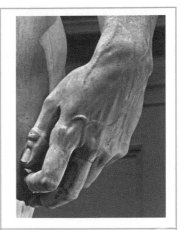

Depth of focus: The human eye, like a camera lens, focuses objects at a specific distance. Objects that are further away or nearer are blurred. This effect provides inexact depth information. It is also called depth of field by photographers.

Sharp images more readily attract the eye than blurred ones, and so degree of blur can be used as a design technique to direct the attention of a viewer.

Reference to nearby known objects: Objects of known sizes provide a reference, against which other objects are judged. Perspective is only a cue to *relative* size, but with a reference object *absolute* size can be judged. Note that although this effect is knowledge-based and not pure geometry like the rest, it is one of the most important cues to distance. The pink cow has been placed next to a boulder in this image of Martian rocks to provide a size reference; it also gives information about distance. It would work even better if the cow had been given a cast shadow to anchor it to the ground.

Image courtesy of Kurt Schwehr and NASA.

Degree of contrast: Because neither air nor water are completely transparent, the contrast between an object and its background *is reduced* as distance increases. Air is relatively clear, and most atmospheric contrast effects only occur when considerable distances are involved. Water, being less transparent, generates larger effects.

Designers can reduce contrast artificially to exaggerate atmospheric contrast and create an enhanced sense of depth. In addition, reducing contrast, like depth of focus or size scaling, can be used to direct attention away from less important objects.

STEREOSCOPIC DEPTH

Some depth cues are not captured in a static image, and are therefore not pictorial. One kind of depth cue comes from the fact that humans, like many other animals, have two front-facing eyes. Visual area 1 contains specialized mechanisms for using the small differences in the images in the two eyes to extract distance information; this ability is called *stereoscopic depth perception.*

Different depth cues have different uses depending on the tasks we are trying to perform. Stereoscopic vision is optimal for *visually guiding our hands* as we reach for nearby objects.[*] It works best in making judgments of the relative distances of *nearby* objects, within a meter or two of our heads. Stereoscopic depth judgments are also most precise for objects that are at *nearly the same depth.* The brain is not good at using stereo information to judge large relative distances. Because of these properties, people who have little or no stereo depth perception (20 percent of the population) still have no difficulty driving cars or walking around, although they will be clumsy when trying to thread needles.

[*]R. Arsenault and C. Ware. 2004. The importance of stereo and eye-coupled perspective for eye-hand coordination in fish tank VR. *Presence: Teleoperators & Virtual Environments.* 13(5): 549-559.

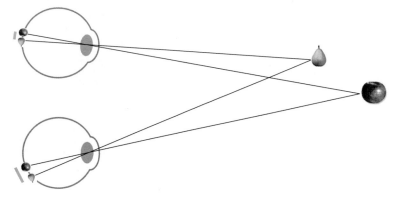

The brain uses differences between the images in the two eyes to determine the relative distance to objects.

Technologies that support stereoscopic viewing present slightly different perspective views of a three-dimensional scene, each based on a slightly different viewpoint.

Stereo technology has, for the most part, been a story of fads that faded, and this is largely because of a failure to understand that the main virtue of stereo vision is the precise guidance of hand movements. The Victorians were fascinated with stereo photos and sold thousands of stereo images. Now they clutter the stands of flea markets. Stereo cameras had a heyday in the 1930s and 1940s but now are almost unobtainable. Many inventors and entrepreneurs have lost their shirts on stereographic movies and television systems in the early 2010s. The problem is that none of these technologies allowed for manual interaction with the visual three-dimensional objects that were represented. If we had virtual three-dimensional environments that allowed us to reach in and move things, then we would appreciate stereo technology more.

STRUCTURE FROM MOTION

Another nonpictorial depth cue that is more useful and powerful than stereoscopic depth is called *structure from motion*. The brain can interpret the moving pattern that arises when objects rotate with respect to a viewpoint to derive information about depth. No special technology is needed beyond simple animation; structure from motion information is provided in conventional movies whenever the camera moves, or whenever an object rotates in the frame of the camera.

It is hardly surprising that structure from motion provides better depth information than stereopsis. Stereoscopic depth comes from just two views, one for each eye. With motion the brain can take advantage of a continuous series of views to interpret depth information.

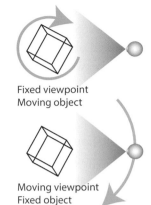

Fixed viewpoint
Moving object

Moving viewpoint
Fixed object

If a rigid three-dimensional computer graphics model, such as this network diagram, is rotated about a vertical axis, its three-dimensional structure will become dramatically more apparent. (Copyright 2002. The Regents of the University of California.)

2.5D DESIGN

2.5D design is a phrase intended to encapsulate a set of design concepts that arise once we start thinking of space in human egocentric coordinates.* The 2.5-dimensional design concept is not new. Low-relief friezes on temples, the Bayeux tapestry, and many medieval manuscript illustrations are 2.5-dimensional designs.

The key idea in 2.5-dimensional design is to treat depth in picture plane very differently from the other two dimensions. Its chief tenets are as follows:

- Depth cues should be used selectively to support design goals. It does not matter if they are combined in ways that are inconsistent with realism.
- Objects should be laid out with minimum occlusion. Usually this means that overall depth in the scene should be limited.

* The term *2.5D design* originates with the work of David Marr who introduced a 2.5D "sketchpad" as one of the stages of visual processing (D. Marr. 1982. *Vision*. Freeman, NY.). However, the specific design principles presented here are not based in any direct way on Marr's theory.

- When occlusion is necessary, ensure critical information is not obscured. Sometimes transparency can help reveal what is behind an occluded object.
- Joints between compound multipart objects should be made clearly visible.
- Make clear spatial relationships, such as *on top of*, *attached to*, and *inside of*.
- Depth should be minimized, but when there are different depths the layout should be carefully designed to make relative distances clear. Simple cast shadows, depth-of-focus effects, and transparency can be used for this.
- Display text in the image plane. Text that is slanted in perspective views is harder to read.
- Give common views of objects for rapid identification.

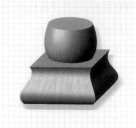

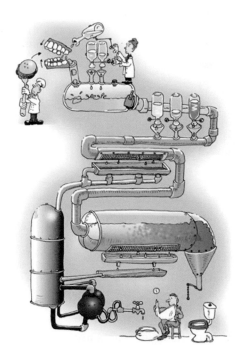

This illustration of the human digestive system is an example of 2.5-dimensional design. Although many of the individual components are rendered in three dimensions, the layout is almost entirely in the picture plane. The connections between components are made very clear. There is occasional occlusion but it never destroys object identity.

(From illustrator David Dickson.)

Note that some of the principles listed previously, particularly the ones relating to joint and object views, are based on concepts that are presented later in Chapter 6. These have been included here to make a more coherent and complete list of 2.5-dimensional design concepts.

HOW MUCH OF THE THIRD DIMENSION?

An important issue in determining whether a three-dimensional or two-dimensional design is appropriate is the nature of what is to be displayed. Some data already has three-dimensional spatial properties; for example, architectural designs, and data from the physical and biological sciences.

On the other hand, many kinds of data and concepts are not inherently spatial. Typical examples are business statistics, social networks, and the myriad of abstract concepts people have developed to cope with the world (education, economic value, causality, to name a few). Some people have tried to use three-dimensional representations for these kinds of things, believing that because we live in a three-dimensional world, three dimensions must be better than two. This argument fails to take into account the fact that we do not perceive three dimensions. Even saying that we perceive 2.5 dimensions is a considerable exaggeration because the information we pick up from the towards-away direction is much less than half of what we get from each of the other two. Attempts to show abstract nonspatial data using three-dimensional views have not been successful, mostly because the information is not displayed clearly and because getting around in three dimensions is much harder than navigation in two dimensions. The cost of getting a good viewpoint in three dimensions is almost always higher than clicking to follow a hypertext link or zooming in two dimensions. This makes visual queries expensive and slows down the cognitive process. Three-dimensional information mazes are especially to be avoided since it takes people a long time to generate a mental map of such a space. On the other hand, a primarily two-dimensional design with a judicious use of depth can be useful because it allows for effective ways of layering information.

Even when designing a truly three-dimensional virtual information space is justified, because the data to be displayed has important three-dimensional properties, 2.5-dimensional design principles should still be applied. Any time we take the viewpoint into account we are making a 2.5-dimensional design decision. This is because the viewpoint affects the visibility of things in the image plane, which is a two-dimensional representation. Often it is useful to mix two-dimensional design elements with three-dimensional design elements. Navigation controls should always be visible on the screen and have a size such that they can be easily selected. Therefore many three-dimensional interfaces actually have two-dimensional controls pasted in the margin. Text labels should be laid out in the image plane, even though they are attached to three-dimensional

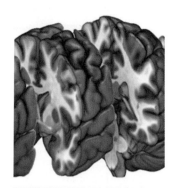

Even though modern scanners produce 3D data imaging the brain, almost all viewing is done with (virtual) 2D slices. Image courtesy of Chris Rordan

98

PPT slide: Introduction

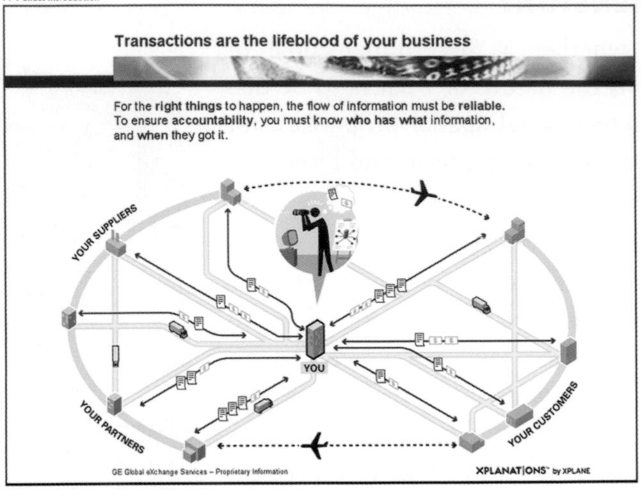

Transactions are the lifeblood of your business

For the **right things** to happen, the flow of information must be **reliable**. To ensure **accountability**, you must know **who has what** information, and **when** they got it.

YOUR SUPPLIERS
YOU
YOUR PARTNERS
YOUR CUSTOMERS

GE Global eXchange Services – Proprietary Information
XPLANAT|ONS™ by XPLANE

PPT slide: The old way (without GXS)

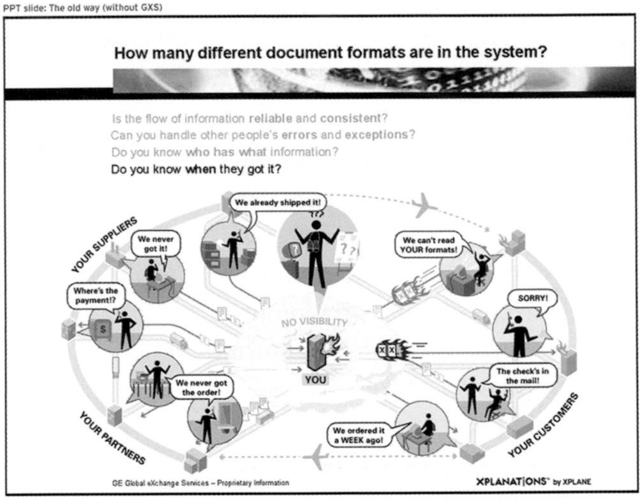

How many different document formats are in the system?

Is the flow of information **reliable** and **consistent**?
Can you handle other people's **errors** and **exceptions**?
Do you know **who has what** information?
Do you know when they got it?

PPT Slide: The new way (with GXS)

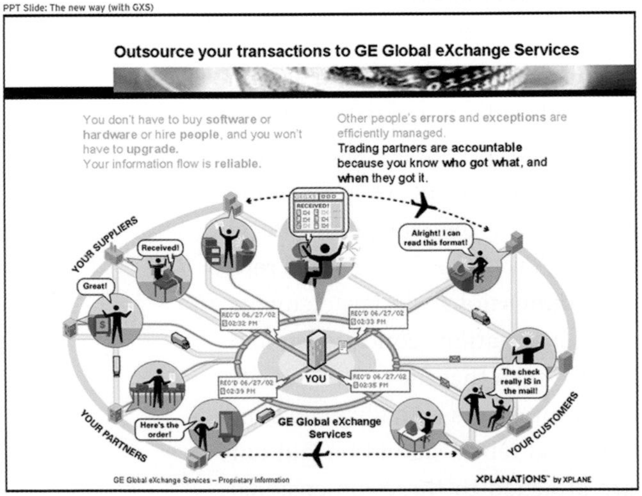

Outsource your transactions to GE Global eXchange Services

This design of a business process was developed by the company XPLANE™ by xplane.com.

It is a good example of the application of 2.5-dimensional design principles to the visualization of a complex business system. It makes careful use of occlusion, height on the picture plane, and layering. No important objects are obscured through occlusion. All the important junctions in the information network are clearly visible.

objects. When designing an interface to a large data space, a two-dimensional overview map should be provided in combination with one or more perspective views showing details. This mitigates the common problems of being lost in a data space. The two-dimensional overview map will be easier to use if it has the same general orientation as the magnified image since people find it difficult to cognitively integrate data seen from radically different viewpoints.

AFFORDANCES

The 2.5-dimensional design principles discussed in the previous pages mostly apply to static, noninteractive designs. They are useful ideas, but they have taken us away from the main thread of this chapter—the connections between perception and action—to which we now return. A useful starting place is the concept of *affordances* developed by the psychologist James Gibson in the 1960s.* Gibson started a revolution in the study of perception by claiming that we perceive physical affordances for actions, and not images on the retina, which had been the basis of prior theories. A flattish and firm ground surface *affords* passage, through walking or running or maneuvering a vehicle. A horizontal surface at waist height *affords* support for objects and tools we are working with. Objects of a certain size, shape, and weight *afford* use as tools. For example, a rock can be substituted for a hammer.

Perception of space is fundamentally about perception of action potential within the local environment. Negative affordances are as important as positive ones since they rule out whole classes of activity. A brick wall is a negative affordance completely ruling out easy access to large areas of space.

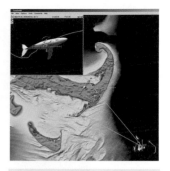

The small inset perspective view of the whale combined with an overview map allows for details to be understood in a spatial context.

* James Gibson's book, *The Senses Considered as Perceptual Systems*, stresses the structure of information in the environment as the foundation of perception.

Boston, Houghton Mifflin. 1966.

A pedestrian perceives the places that afford safe walking. A driver perceives the places that afford vehicle navigation. Buildings provide the negative affordances in that they restrict travel. On the other hand, if a pedestrian's goal is shopping for shoes then affordances relating to the likely presence of shoe stores will be perceived.

Gibson conceived affordances as *physical properties of the environment*, but in reality many of the most useful affordances have to do with access to information. To make the concept of affordances more broadly applicable, computer interface designers have changed its meaning. As it is used now, it has a cognitive dimension that departs from Gibson's definition. *Cognitive affordances* are readily perceived *possibilities for action*. For example, a computer interface may have a number of on-screen buttons that are available for metaphorically pressing with the mouse cursor.

This office space, although appearing messy, is well structured for cognitive work. The computer is the nearest object to the worker and at the focus of attention. Other information-carrying objects are papers arranged so that the most important are close to hand and near the tops of piles. Less frequently accessed sources of information, such as books, are more distant. The work space has affordances structured for efficient access to information.

THE WHERE PATHWAY

Affordances are ultimately about linking *perception and action*, and there are pathways in the brain that are specialized for this task. The *where* pathway runs forward from V1 and V2 to the parietal lobe in the middle of the upper part of the brain. The parietal lobe contains a number of coarse *action maps* of visual space. There are maps with retinal coordinates, body coordinates, and external world coordinates. Each map links visual information to some form of guided movement. The lateral intraparietal (LIP) region has a representation of visual space in retinal coordinates, with areas weighed based on attentional priority. LIP is critically involved with planning the next eye movement. The medial intraparietal (MIP) region contains another distinct representation of nearby space that is used to guide arm movements. Other regions provide a head-centered representation of space and a body-centered representation of space, used for locomotion. Each of these regions has strong onward connections to the motor cortex—a part of the brain involved in setting up the sequence of muscle contractions needed to set part of the body in motion.

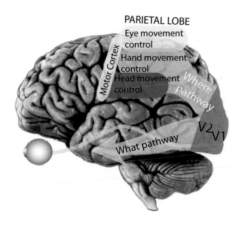

PARIETAL LOBE
Eye movement control
Hand movement control
Head movement control
Motor Cortex
Where pathway
What pathway
V2 V1

The parietal lobe is the upper-central part of the cortex. It contains pathways that link vision to action.

Various maps of visual space are contained in the parietal lobe, each supporting a different kind of action pathway. These regions are actually much smaller than shown on this diagram.

The use of the term "map" in the preceding description implies something rather static, detailed, and permanent. This is misleading because these maps are, in fact, temporary and have very little detail. For example, the eye-space map is updated every time we move our eyes. It contains a rough representation of the locations of a few objects in space that are task-relevant. These representations function to support the activities we are currently engaged in, and they contain just enough information for those actions.

Much of what goes on in the *where* pathway is unconscious. Most of the time, we are completely unaware that we are making eye movements. We are also unaware of the hand movements we make in grasping moving things. When we walk on rough ground, we constantly adjust our foot placements without conscious attention. Our motor-planning system registers the presence of small obstacles, adjusts the spacing of our footsteps, and sets off a train of signals to muscles that cause our foot placement to change by just the right amount.

A basic ability to move our eyes to a simple target is probably innate, although it becomes much more skilled with time. But other visually guided movements must be learned from scratch, often with consider-able effort.[*] Visual motor skills, such as walking, reaching for an object, driving a car, or playing golf, go through well-documented stages, from being extremely difficult and demanding complete attention to effortless and being done automatically. Increasing levels of skill means that the pathways linking perception and action are stronger and require less and less high-level attention. Baseball players have highly developed pathways specialized for catching or hitting fast-moving balls. Teenagers who play videogames for hundreds or thousands of hours have highly developed visual-motor pathways for navigating through artificial three-dimensional spaces. These pathways are optimized, mapping the specific configura-tion of buttons found in game controllers into movements through virtual computer graphics–generated spaces.

ARTIFICIAL INTERACTIVE SPACES

In interactive video games, the critical affordances are artificial, and in a sense, metaphoric. Because our mental models of space and gravity come first from the physical world, we assume that objects in the virtual world of computer games will stay on tabletops. The real is a metaphor that guides the design of the artificial.

It is only necessary for things to exhibit *roughly* the right physical behavior for objects to appear normal when we interact with them. For example, the way balls ricochet from each other can be altered in ways that substantially distort physical laws and people will not notice. Vision researchers call this *the naïve physics of perception*. It means that the models that are embedded in our nervous systems are only crude approx-imate representations of physical reaction patterns. One consequence of this is that we can make virtual worlds of video games in which the basics of physics are distorted without people noticing. Video games often dis-tort the physics of action and reaction in extreme ways and even when we do notice we can very rapidly adapt to such distortion so long as the pattern linking perception and action is preserved. For example, game designers usually reduce the force of gravity by a factor of two or more and still players are able to control the characters with little or no diffi-culty even though they jump higher and fall more slowly than they should according to strict realism.

[*]Elizabeth Spelke and her co-workers at Cornell University measured babies' looking behaviors, and used the results to argue that we are not born with an innate appreciation for gravity, although we are born with an appreciation for the permanence and solidity of objects.

Spelke, E.S., Breinlinger, K., Macomber, J., and Jacobsen, K, 1992. Origins of Knowledge, Psychological Review. vol 99(4), 605–632.

Efficient designs for information access generally build on visual motor skills we already possess. For example, although a computer mouse is completely disconnected from the cursor on the screen, the cursor moves to the right when we move our hand to the right. This builds on the very early skills a baby develops when initially random hand movement cause objects in the visual field to move. Try rotating your mouse 90 degrees and selecting some object on your screen to see how difficult things can be when we violate the basic correspondence between hand movement and cursor movement.

The idea that our mental models of space perception are grounded in real-world interaction requires some qualification. The neural architecture and the most basic human capabilities are innate. But the world is changing in profound ways. As younger and younger children work with computers, purely invented consequences of actions, such as cursors that move with the mouse, become basic. Pull-down menus are common and have come to be as real in an important way as physical balls that roll when kicked. With extended use, the motor pathways that connect perception to action can become just as strong for the computer interaction as for the physical action.

As natural as walking?

Many individuals spend significant parts of their lives interacting with computers containing simulated environments. If these virtual worlds contain virtual laws that differ substantially from the real world, then these patterns will become the basis for an alternative naïve physics, not based on the real world, but upon artificial worlds. Human perception is, over time, becoming less grounded in real-world interactions. Skill with a computer mouse is already assumed for computer-interface designers. Skill with common video game controllers is becoming increasingly ubiquitous.

SPACE TRAVERSAL AND COGNITIVE COSTS

We now return to the point that moving through space can be regarded as a cognitive cost. We weigh the time to go to the library against the time to access information online, taking into account the relative quality of information we are likely to get. There are cognitive tradeoffs other than time to consider. We choose to travel by train, as opposed to driving a car, because we can read and write while on the train but not in the car, although even on the train the work we can do is far less than we can accomplish in an office that is highly optimized for cognitive work.

In this light, it is useful to review the basic costs of some common modes of information access. A list of rough values for various costs is set out in the following table. Some designers of computer interfaces literally count such costs for the execution of a particular task—how many mouse movements, how many eye movements, how many key strokes, and so on. In this way, the efficiency of one design can be compared against another. The table is far too rough an approximation to be used for this purpose. Rather it is intended as food for thought. A computer interface design can often be dramatically improved by changes that involve, for example, making it possible to access a frequently used piece of information via an eye movement instead of a mouse movement. Although pure cognitive efficiency is never the only design issue, it is always something that should be taken into account.

Internal pattern comparison	0.04 second	Occurs whenever our eyes alight.
Eye movements	0.1 second	Tightly coupled with visual cognitive system.
Mouse hover: A hover query is what occurs when the cursor is placed over an information object and information appears. No clicking is required.	1.0 second	If they are highly optimized, hover queries can be invaluable techniques for rapid exploration. As the mouse cursor moves over a particular object, related data objects become highlighted
Mouse select	1.5 seconds	A mouse selection of a web link can cause an entirely new page of information to appear.
Zooming: Discussed shortly	$Dist = 4x^t$ (seconds)	The most efficient way of traversing large distances with visual continuity.
Walk	4 kph/dist (minutes)	Good affordances for contemplative thought. Poor affordances for interactive cognitive work.
Drive	80 kph/dist (minutes-hours)	Moderate affordances for contemplative thought. Poor affordances for interactive cognitive work.
Fly	400 kph/dist (hours)	Moderate affordances for contemplative thought. Depending on class of travel moderate affordances for interactive cognitive work.
Train	100 kph/dist (hours)	Moderate affordances for contemplative thought. Depending on class of travel moderate affordances for interactive cognitive work.

The advent of high-performance three-dimensional computer graphics has led to the invention of navigation methods that are nonmetaphoric in that they are not based on real-world interactions. One of these is the zooming interface. As it is usually implemented (for example, in Google Earth), zooming causes a constant change in scale per unit time. If we are zooming in, in one second we might see objects four times as big. In two seconds, we will be able to see four times as big again, or sixteen times in total. In three seconds, we can see $4 \times 4 \times 4$, or sixty-four times the detail. At this rate, we can zoom from an overview of the entire earth showing down to a view of a person's hand, in about 14 seconds. Fourteen more seconds will get us down to the size of a single molecule. This is the power of exponential change.

Smooth zooming at a rate of four times per second will still give perfect visual continuity.

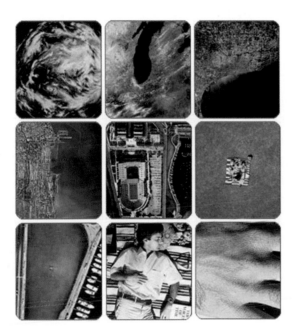

Part of the extraordinary image sequence created by Charles and Ray Eames, showing a spiraling in from space to a point on earth.

The hyperlink is another example of a new nonmetaphoric method of navigating information spaces. The click of a mouse button selecting an object on one screen causes a new screen of information, sometimes from across the world, to appear in less than a second. Interface techniques such as zooming and hyperlinks are causing such radical changes in the cost of navigating information spaces that human society is being altered. Because information access is increasingly no longer a matter of traversing physical space, students rarely go to libraries, people meet one another online, and gamblers can avoid casinos.

CONCLUSION

The main point of this chapter has been that the functional aesthetics of space are related to the cost of accessing information. Although we live in three dimensions, we always see the world from a particular viewpoint, and it is always faster to redirect our gaze to get new information than to move our heads or our whole bodies. Perceptual space is also flattened in terms of its information content, with much less information being rapidly available in the towards-away (depth) direction than the sideways and up-down because we cannot see through most objects. The pattern-processing mechanisms of the brain operate on the two-dimensional retinal image, which means that two-dimensional image plane information is analyzed much more efficiently than depth information.

This is not to deny depth perception, but depth is perceived in ways that are radically different from the way patterns in the image plane are perceived. The brain determines relative distance by means of depth cues such as occlusion, shape from shading, and linear perspective. Information from the depth cues is used in a piecemeal fashion to help perform the task at hand. Sometimes motion parallax will be most important, sometimes relative size and sometimes shading information, it all depends on what we are trying to accomplish.

The set of design principles that takes the space-time structure of perception into account is called 2.5-dimensional design. The fact that the brain is capable of interpreting depth cues in a piecemeal fashion frees the designer to break the rules of perspective and make use of depth cues in different combinations as they seem most suitable to serve the purposes of a design. There is no need to use them all together in a consistent way unless visual realism is, in and of itself, a design goal. The piecemeal use of depth cues is part of the 2.5-dimensional design; however, the layout of objects and patterns as they appear in the image plane should be the primary design consideration.

The designer of interactive computer-based applications has options relating to the cost of information access. The cost of eye movements can be compared together with the cost of a mouse click. The cost of virtually walking can be compared to the cost of flying or zooming. Having an understanding of the various tradeoffs involved in making these choices is critical in designing effective cognitive tools.

Chapter 6

Visual Objects, Words, and Meaning

The image of a naked nine-year-old Vietnamese girl Phan Thi Kim Phuc running from her napalmed and burning village in the background gained a Pulitzer Prize for the photographer Nick Ut and helped turn public opinion further against the Vietnam War on June 8, 1972. Images can evoke very rapid and powerful emotional responses. The activation of meaning from an image generally occurs in a small fraction of a second, much less time than it takes to read a paragraph of text. This activation through a single glance makes images far more efficient than words at conveying certain kinds of information.

In this chapter, we examine the brain processes involved in object and scene perception and consider the links between visual and nonvisual (especially verbal) information. We shall begin with an overview of the neurophysiology, and end with a discussion of the role of images in obsessive thinking.

Visual Thinking for Information Design. DOI: https://doi.org/10.1016/B978-0-12-823567-6.00006-9

THE INFEROTEMPORAL CORTEX AND THE WHAT CHANNEL

We have already discussed the processing of increasingly complex patterns through brain areas, V1, V2, V4, and lateral occipital cortex. Now we move up to the stage of the inferotemporal (IT) cortex, where we will encounter patterns that are meaningful in an everyday sense.

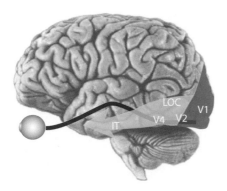

The "what" channel consists of a series of strongly interconnected brain areas that contain neurons responding to progressively more complex patterns. At the end of the chain is the inferotemporal (IT) cortex.

The IT cortex is an area at each side of the brain (behind the temples) containing neurons specialized for complex visual patterns corresponding to recognizable objects and scenes. It contains a number of subareas. There is, for example, a subregion called the fusiform gyrus that contains cells responding specifically to faces. Other regions are specialized for cars and houses. There are also links to areas in the forebrain and the midbrain that provide *multimodal* connections between visual information and information processed by other sensory channels.

In order to recognize objects and scenes, the brain must solve a number of very difficult problems. Consider face recognition; studies of human pattern perception show that humans are much better at identifying objects when the viewpoint is a familiar one. Finding a face in an upside-down picture of a crowd is difficult.

Identifying the famous faces on the *Sgt. Pepper's Lonely Hearts Club Band* album cover is much harder when they are inverted.

Spatial memory for scenes is also viewpoint specific. Suppose someone has always entered a room from a particular door and has always stayed in that room near to that entrance so they have never experienced it from a substantially different viewpoint. Generally they will fail to recognize the room when entering from a door on the opposite side. We can still recognize objects and scenes when there are quite large variations in the viewpoint from which we see them; the difficulties occur only with extreme changes of view. What applies to scenes also applies to individual objects. As a rule of thumb, we can rotate an object by about 20 degrees and scale it by a factor of two or three and still identify it rapidly. How does the brain do it?

GENERALIZED VIEWS FROM PATTERNS

The IT object identification areas receive bottom-up information from the V4 pattern processing region. V4 neurons are capable of responding to patterns that are rotated and distorted in variations of a prototype.

A neuron in area V4 might respond to all of these pattern variations.

But a pattern cannot be rotated or distorted too much or the neuron will stop responding. This tolerance of distortion makes the task of the IT cortex much easier. Complex objects, such as human faces, cats, teapots, or automobiles (all things that neurons in the IT cortex are likely to be sensitive to) can be thought of as patterns of patterns. The identifiable object patterns are constructed from simpler V4 patterns, which in turn are made up of elementary pattern components coming from V1 and V2.[*] In order to identify a face, for example, several sets of neurons must respond to a few *generalized views* such as a full face view, a three-quarters view, and a profile view. Each of these views provides a quite distinct visual pattern of patterns. Most other views of a person's face will provide only minor variations of one of these generalized views. Because the component pattern recognizers are tolerant of distortion, the overall mechanism is too.

[*]Neuroscience has yet to decide whether it is single neurons or assemblages of neurons that fulfill this function.

A face is a pattern of patterns

Some theorists, beginning with the philosopher Plato, have held that we recognize objects with reference to other objects that are somehow *canonical*, abstract ideal forms. Superficially, the generalized views mentioned earlier might seem like a similar idea. This is not at all what is intended. We recognize faces and other things because clusters of neurons that receive inputs from other clusters of neurons respond strongly when a certain face becomes imaged on the retina. This is not a matching process, and there is no idealized form, simply a learned response to a range of patterns.

STRUCTURED OBJECTS

There has been an intense theoretical debate in the community of vision researchers as to whether or not we have three-dimensional "models" in our heads.• Most of the evidence suggests that most of us do not and that the "generalized views" account of recognition is sufficient to explain how people normally perceive objects in most cases. There are exceptions; for instance, people like carpenters and engineers develop specialized skills to mentally manipulate 3D structures. Such people do have some limited ability to build models in their head, albeit quite simple ones. The fact that there are very large individual differences in this skill suggests that it is not basic to all perception.

•A model in the head would be a neural representation of the three-dimensional spatial layout of an object's parts.

Nevertheless, there is clear evidence that we all have some limited ability to perceive the three-dimensional structure of objects. For some objects composed of component parts, the way those parts are connected is critical.

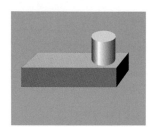 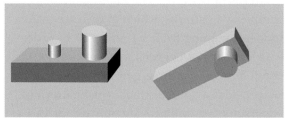

If asked which object in the blue box matches the one in the pink box most people will choose the one on the right. But according to the theory of object perception, based on two-dimensional generalized views, the one on the left of the blue box should be chosen because the image is mostly identical.

In order to account for our ability to identify structured objects, Irving Biederman proposed the *geon* theory.• This is the idea that the brain contains mechanisms to identify three-dimensional structural components of objects that he calls geons. Geons, in his theory, are three-dimensional shapes such as cones and cylinders that can be curved or straight. The brain stores information about the geon components of objects, together

•I. Biederman, 1987. Recognition by components: A theory of human image understanding. *Psychological Review.* 92(2): 115–147.

with a description of the way they are connected—a kind of structural skeleton. When the object we see is a horse, the geons are its four legs, each composed of sub-geons, its head, its neck, and its tail. The way these parts are connected form the geon skeleton.

A geon problem !

The geon theory is probably the most controversial of the theories that are discussed here. Few researchers believe that neurons respond to exactly the set of three-dimensional primitives that Biederman proposed. However, there is strong evidence that we perceive the way parts of objects are interconnected—the structural skeleton in Biederman's theory. Objects can be identified far more rapidly if they are presented in views that clearly reveal the connections between component parts. For this reason, in design, it is always a good idea to make the connection points between parts of objects as clear as possible.

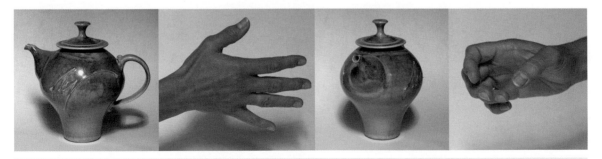

In the left-hand pair of images, the critical connections between the parts of both the teapot and the hand are evident in the silhouette. In the right hand pair these connections are not as clearly shown and in the case of the teapot the handle is invisible. The right-hand pair is less likely to be identified correctly from a brief presentation.

There is no reason for the brain to have only a single process for object identification, and it is likely that both the generalized two-dimensional views theory and the structured object theory are correct. The brain appears to do most identification through the mechanism of two-dimensional patterns, but for certain kinds of objects a kind of higher-level structural analysis of the kind Biederman proposed may provide the most critical information. Both theories suggest ways of making clear graphic representations.

GIST AND SCENE PERCEPTION

Identifying scenes provides another kind of problem for the visual system. People can easily identify scenes, such as "a busy road," "a rural landscape," or "a fast-food restaurant," and they can make this kind of categorical judgment in less than a tenth of a second even if they have never seen that particular road, landscape, or restaurant before. This is about the same time it takes for a person to identify that an object is a person, a dog, a car, or belonging to some generic class. This rapid identification is a problem for traditional theories of scene perception because they held that a scene is identified by means of the objects it contains, which implied that objects would have to be recognized first and faster than the scene as a whole.

We can get the gist of a scene in less than a tenth of a second. This is as fast as we can identify individual objects.

The rapid characterization of a scene is called getting its *gist*. Neither the generalized two-dimensional views theory nor the structured object recognition theory can account for why it is so rapid and efficient. Gist perception can, nevertheless, be thought of as another example of a process whereby patterns of patterns are the key. Two researchers at the Massachusetts Institute of Technology, Antonio Torralba and Aude Oliva, have sketched out how this might occur.[*] They showed how common scenes have typical spatial feature components, distributed in characteristic ways. These can include large-scale pattern arrangements of patches of

[*]A. Oliva and A. Torralba. 2006. Building the gist of a scene: The role of global image features in recognition. *Progress in Brain Research*. 155: 527–532.

textures and colors. There is no need for objects to be identified for a scene to be recognized. For example, beach scenes are generally characterized by a large blue area at the top of the image (the sky) with striated white and blue gray areas either to the left or the right of the image (the sea with waves), and a large beige area (sand) containing smaller vertical and horizontals shapes (people) on the remaining side. Recognizing such patterns of patterns is exactly the kind of thing that neurons in the IT cortex are good at.

This is the average of hundreds of pictures containing a person, all taken in Mallorca, Spain.

Notice that even though there are no individual small-scale features present, it is clear that there is a standing person in an exterior environment with a quite flat terrain. It is not necessary to recognize objects to perceive the scene.

A. Oliva and A. Torralba. 2007. Building the gist of a scene: The role of global image features in recognition. Progress in *Brain Research*, 155: 527–532.

The statistical properties of a mediaeval cityscape are represented here.

The statistical properties of a beach scene are represented here.

Scene gist can powerfully influence how we see an object embedded in a scene. In the blurred street scene below left, there is an automobile visible on the street. In the picture below right, a bottle is standing on the table. Closer evaluation reveals these two blobby objects to be the same.[*]

[*]A. Torralba, 2003. Context priming for object detection. *International Journal of Computer Vision*. 53(2): 169–191.

Although they seem very different, objects and scenes can be thought of as high-level patterns; both consist of patterns of patterns. The IT cortex has numerous specialized object identification subregions, each of which has developed to process a different class of objects or scenes. These pattern-processing clusters develop through our lifetimes reflecting our visual skill development. The more we need to be able to appreciate certain kinds of visual signs the more neurons become recruited to that task and the more tuned they become to specific patterns that are meaningful to us. The process starts when we are babies, and it never stops. Some specialists, including race car drivers, visual designers, chefs, dance critics, and those who fly fish, continue to develop and refine very specialized pattern identification skills.

VISUAL AND VERBAL WORKING MEMORY

Up to this point, we have been discussing objects and scenes as pure visual entities. But scenes and objects have meaning largely through links to other kinds of information stored in a variety of specialized regions of the brain. This information includes the predictive neural models introduced in Chapter 1 and elaborated in Chapter 8. Partly these consist of action patterns, eye-movement scanning strategies, and semantic content stored in the language systems of the brain. These links become activated through the operation of high-level attention-guiding mechanisms that are called *working memories*.

The operative term in *working memory* is *work*, not memory. Information is only held in working memory from between one-tenth of a second and, at most, a few seconds, and it is only held to support some ongoing cognitive process. An entity in visual working memory can be thought of as a temporary grouping or *nexus*, whereby links are formed between active visual patterns derived from the visual image on the retina scene information and information relating to nonvisual stored meanings. With cognitive work, the most important of the nonvisual links is information held in verbal working memory.•

•The account given here has a number of sources. The term nexus describing a temporary binding together of information comes from R.A. Rensink. 2000. The dynamic representation of scenes. *Visual cognition*. 7: 17–42. But the idea also has roots in the concept of a cognitive *object file* developed earlier by D. Kahneman and A. Triesman, 1992. The reviewing of object files: Object specific integration of information. *Cognitive Psychology*. 24: 175–219.

VERBAL WORKING MEMORY

The brain has a specialized set of neural subsystems that process language. These are situated in parts of the brain that are separate and distinct from the visual processing subsystems. They include Wernicke's area, where language is interpreted, and Broca's area, where speech is produced. Verbal working memory, like visual working memory, is a temporary transitory store.

Verbal working memory can hold about *two seconds* worth of speech information in what is sometimes called an *echoic loop*. It is also useful to think of this as about three chunks of information. Much of what is conventionally taken to be "thinking," namely the internal monologue that we sometimes become aware of, is a form of internalized speech also occurring in verbal working memory. Because of this our ability to think and simultaneously listen to the speech of others is limited.

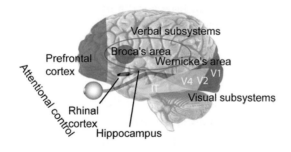

CONTROL OF THE ATTENTION AND THE COGNITIVE PROCESS

Information in visual and verbal working memory is often temporarily bound together. A visual chunk may be momentarily bound to a verbal chunk. The image of a stray cat and the phrase "get it out of here" become combined. Other temporary bindings are also formed. Visual chunks may be trigger eye-movement plans and cognitive action plans needed to execute the next few mental operations. A plan is formed to chase the cat. These temporary bindings can be thought of as acts of attention, the shifting focus of the mind.

The prefrontal cortex has long been considered critical to the temporary bindings that occur as part of more complex plans. In the words of neuroscientists Earl Miller and Jonathan Cohen, *"Cognitive control stems from the active maintenance of patterns of activity in the prefrontal cortex that represent goals and the means to achieve them. They provide bias signals to other brain structures whose net effect is to guide the flow of activity along neural pathways that establish the proper mappings between inputs, internal states, and outputs needed to perform a given task."*[*]

[*]E.F. Miller and J.D. Cohen, 2001. An integrative theory of prefrontal cortex function. *Annual Review of Neuroscience*. 24: 167–202.

GETTING INTO VISUAL WORKING MEMORY

We are now in a position to sketch out the entire process whereby a visual object comes to be represented in the mind. Of course, the cognitive process is ongoing; what we have just seen influences where we will look next and the information we pull out of the retinal image. In turn, that information influences where we will look next, and so on.

But we must start somewhere, so we will start, arbitrarily, at the bottom. The information (biased by attentional tuning as described in Chapter 2) sweeps up through the various stages of the *what* hierarchy, retina→V1→V2→V4→IT, with more and more complex patterns being formed at each level. The simple features of V1 and V2 become continuous contours and specific shapes in V4. More complex patterns are activated in specialized regions of the IT cortex that correspond to meaningful objects we have experienced in our lifetimes.

When the wave of activation reaches the IT cortex *all* similar patterns are activated, although by differing amounts depending on how good a fit there is between the image information and the particular pattern detection unit. For example, if we are seeing the front of a person's face all stored patterns corresponding to frontally viewed faces will be activated, only some more than others depending on the degree of match. Ongoing cognitive activities will also have an influence. For example, looking for a particular person will prime those patterns that have links to other information already in verbal working memory about that person. Those patterns that have been primed will be more readily activated than those that have not.

Many patterns become activated to some extent in the IT cortex, but we actually perceive only very few. A second wave of activation, this time from the top-down, determines which of the many patterns actually makes it into working memory. At this point, a kind of neural choice occurs and so we perceive not all faces but the face of a particular person. The selection process is based on the pattern that is responded to most strongly. This is called a *biased competition model*.[*] The biasing has to do

[*]Many theorists have developed variations on the biased competition idea. See, for example, E. Miller, 2000. The prefrontal cortex and cognitive control. *Nature Reviews: Neuroscience*. 1: 59–65.

with priming and the task relevance of the visual information. Many patterns compete, but only between one and three win. Winning means that all competing pattern matches to other faces are suppressed. The result of winning is that a top-down wave of activation both enhances those lower-level patterns and suppresses all other pattern components.

The overall result is a nexus binding together the particular V4 patterns that make up the winning objects. Only one to three visual objects make the cut and are held in visual working memory.

Those visual objects that win will generally be linked to other information that is nonvisual. Relevant concepts may become active in verbal working memory; action sequences (part of executable predictive long-term memories) controlling the eyes or the hands may be activated or brought to a state of readiness.

How fast can we extract objects from a visual image? In an experiment carried out in 1969 at MIT, psychologist Mary Potter and her research assistant Ellen Levy presented images to people at various rates.[*] They were asked to press a button if they saw some specific object in a picture, for example, a dog. They found that they could flash a sequence of pictures, sometimes with one containing a dog, at rates of up to ten per second and still people would guess its presence correctly most of the time. But this does not mean that they could remember much from the pictures. On the contrary, they could remember almost nothing, just that there was a dog present. It does, however, establish an upper rate for the identification of individual objects. As a general rule of thumb, between one and three objects are rapidly identified each time the eye alights and rests at each fixation point usually for about one-fifth of a second. Even when we study individual objects closely, this typically involves a series of fixations on different parts of the object to pick out specific features, not a prolonged fixation.

[*]M.C. Potter and E. Levy, 1969. Recognition memory for a rapid sequence of pictures. *Journal of Experimental Psychology.* 81: 10–15. The technique of rapidly presenting image sequences is called RSVP for *Rapid Serial Visual Presentation.*

THINKING IN ACTION: RECEIVING A CUP OF COFFEE

To put some flesh on these rather abstract bones consider this example of visual thinking in action. Suppose we are being given a cup of coffee by a new acquaintance at a social gathering. There are a number of visual tasks being executed. The most pressing is the hand coordination needed to reach for and grasp the cup by the handle. Fixation is directed at the handle, and the handle is one of the objects that makes it into visual working memory. In this context the meaning of the handle has to do with its graspability and a link is formed to a motor sequence required to reach for and grasp the handle. The location of the other person's hand and its predicted trajectory is also critical because we must coordinate our actions with theirs and thus some information about the hand makes it into visual working memory. This makes two visual working memory objects.

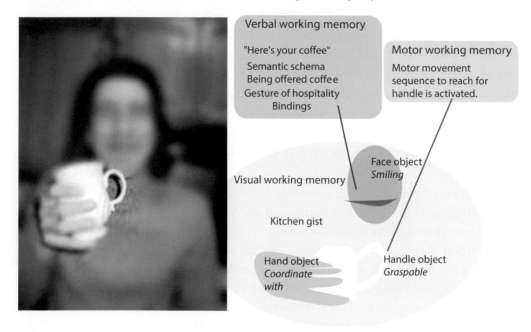

Our fixation immediately prior to the present one was directed to the face of the acquaintance and this information is retained as a third visual working memory object. Face information has links to verbal working memory, information important for the dialogue we are engaged in. The visual working memory objects also have links to several action plans. One plan involves the motor sequence required to grasp the handle. Another plan schedules the next eye movement. Once the handle has been grasped, the eye will be directed back to the face. Yet another plan is concerned with the maintenance of the conversation. None of these plans are very elaborate, very little is held in each of the working memories, but what is held is exactly what is important for us to carry out this social dialogue that includes the receipt of a mug of coffee. The whole thing can be thought of as a loosely coupled network of temporarily active processes, a kind of dance of meaning.

ELABORATIONS AND IMPLICATIONS FOR DESIGN

We now have the outline of what it means to have a visual object in mind. The remainder of this chapter is devoted to elaborating parts of this theory and discussing some of its implications for design.

MAKE OBJECTS EASY TO IDENTIFY

The theory of objects as patterns of patterns means that some objects will be easier to identify than others. The most typical exemplars of an object class are identified faster because the corresponding visual patterns are more strongly encoded. We will be able to see that a member of the Labrador breed is a dog faster than we can identify a Daschund or a Doberman.

This view of a low-relief carving in the Kom Ombo Temple in Egypt has figures arranged so that all their important parts are visible. Hands, feet, heads, and shoulders are all given in stereotyped views. Likewise, the connections between these components are all clear. (Image from Suresh Krishna.)

There are also views that are more canonical. These include both typical views and views that show critical relationships between structural parts. Showing the joints clearly in a structured object will make it easier to identify that object. This can be done by posing the object in such a way that the joints are clear in the silhouette, as is common in some Egyptian low-relief carvings. It can also be done by selecting a viewpoint that makes the critical joints and component parts clear.

NOVELTY

Humans have come to dominate the world partly because of our curiosity. Seeking visual novelty is one of the fundamental abilities of newborns.♦ In later life we continue to actively seek novelty, either to exploit it to our advantage, or to avoid it if it presents a danger. Novelty seeking manifests itself when we are not intensely focused on some cognitive agenda. At such times people use their free cognitive cycles to scan their environments, seeking mental stimulation. We are usually not aware that we are doing this.

♦Novelty seeking in babies is so strong that it has become one of the basic tools used to understand the perceptual capacities of the very young. For example, this method has been used to show that an understanding of the *persistence of objects* seems to be innate. Babies are most curious about objects that disappear, or reappear without cause. They look longer at novel objects. E. Spelkey, et al. 1992. Origins of knowledge. *Psychological Review*. 99: 605–632.

This provides an opportunity for the advertiser. Because image gist is processed rapidly, providing an image in an advertisement ensures that at least some information will be processed on the first glance. Holding the viewer's attention can be achieved through novelty. One method for triggering further exploratory cognitive activity is by creating a strong gist-object conflict. If a scene with clearly expressed gist is combined with an object that is incompatible with that gist the result will be a cognitive effort to resolve the conflict in some way. The advertiser may thereby capture a few more cognitive cycles.

The novel view of the Earth rising over the surface of the Moon transposes an image that is familiar (the moon rising over the Earth's horizon) in a way that is visually surprising and deeply thought provoking. This photograph taken in lunar orbit by astronaut William Anders in 1968 has been called the most influential environmental photograph ever taken; it is credited to awakening people to the fragility and isolation of our planet.

Gist-object mismatches are easy to create and can be as straightforward as putting someone in her underwear in a room full of suits, although the novelty of this particular device is fast wearing off. Computer tools such as Adobe Photoshop make it almost trivial to add an object to a scene. The trick is to add some witty twist and at the same time get people think of some product in a more positive light. Gist-object mismatch is actually an old device that has been used by artists throughout the centuries. The technique became the dominant method of the twentieth-century surrealist painters such as Rene Magritte (men in suits falling from the sky, a train emerging from a fireplace) and Salvador Dalí (soft clocks melting from trees, a woman with desk drawers emerging from her body).

Another way of holding attention is to create a visual puzzle. The image on the facing page, created by London photographer Tim Flach, uses an extreme form of non-canonical view to accomplish this. Because of the view, gist perception will not be immediate, although there is probably enough information to discern that the image is of animate forms. The strong, unfamiliar outlines of the forms will be enough to capture a second glance and further exploration will likely ensue.

IMAGES AS SYMBOLS

Some graphic symbols function in much the same way as words. They have commonly agreed on meanings. Examples are "stop" and "yield" traffic signs. Many religious symbols have become embedded in our visual culture. What is important about these symbols is that the visual shapes have become cognitively bound to a particular nonvisual cluster of concepts. Viewing these symbols causes an automatic and rapid activation of these concepts, although the degree to which this occurs will depend on the cognitive activity of the moment.

Symbols with the ability to trigger particular associations can have huge value. Companies often spend vast amounts in getting their symbols to the state of automatic recognition by a large proportion of the population. In extreme examples, such as soft drinks manufacturing, the value of the company is closely linked to the value of the company's symbol. Coca Cola has been estimated to be worth thirty-three billion dollars. Most of that is branding. Producing cola for a few cents a bottle is easy. What is difficult is getting people to pay $2.00 for it. Coca Cola's famous trademark itself is estimated to be worth more than ten billion dollars.

There is a conflict between the need of advertisers to provide novelty in order to capture the attention of potential buyers, and the need to be consistent to establish a well-defined brand image. Companies can only change a logo at huge cost and with enormous care and planning. Generally it is much safer to improvise variations on an old symbol than to establish a new one. This allows for attention-grabbing novelty, while maintaining that all-important instant brand recognition.

The poster for the movie *Walk the Line*, advertising a biography of country and western singer, Johnny Cash, is full of images that function as symbols. The guitar symbolizes that its wearer is a musician. The particular shape of the finger plate denotes the country and western style. The flames in the background symbolize the personal torment of the singer and also a famous Cash song "Ring of Fire." The vertical bar symbolizes the title of another song, also given in words, "Walk the Line." For anyone already somewhat familiar with the life and work of Johnny Cash, the poster will automatically trigger these rich layers of meaning.

MEANING AND EMOTION

Certain kinds of scenes and objects have strong emotive associations. Some are universal. Most people have positive associations for cute children and animals. But many other images have far more varied individual associations. For one person an image of a lake might be associated with good times at the family cottage. For another, the lake might be a foreign place evoking discomfort, lack of sanitation, and insects.

Mothers and children have positive associations for almost everyone. Such images can be used to support messages about family values, heath care products, or the need for education.

Beyond the most superficial level, understanding a communication requires cognitive effort and unless people have strong self-motivation, information will not be attended and therefore not processed. Without some emotional valence many presentations will not be effective simply because the audience will not care. Adding emotive images can turn a disinterested audience into an attentive audience.

A message about the danger to humpback whales from ship strikes is far more likely to result in actions and donations if accompanied by images such as this. It shows a whale killed by a ship's propeller.

IMAGERY AND DESIRE

Mental imagery often accompanies feelings of desire. Daydreams about food, sex, material goods, or experiences such as laying on the beach consist, in large part, of a stream of mental imagery. In a paper, entitled "Imagery, Relish and Exquisite Torture," a group of researchers from the University of Queensland in Australia and the University of Sheffield in England set out a theory of how the process works.[*] They argue that imagery provides a short-term form of relief for a psychological deficit. Unfortunately, the effect is short-lived and a heightened sense of deficit results. This leads to more imagery-seeking behavior. The effect is something like scratching an itch. At first it helps, but a short time later the itch is worst and more scratching results. The imagery involved can be either internal, purely in the mind, or external, from magazines or web pages. An important point is that the process can be started with external imagery. Their studies also suggested a way of getting out of this cycle of imagery-mediated obsession. Having people carry out cognitive tasks using alternative imagery, unrelated to the object of desire, was effective in reducing cravings.

[*]D.J. Kavanagh, J. Andrade, and J. May, 2005. Imagery, relish and exquisite torture: The elaborated intrusion theory of desire. *Psychological Review.* 112: 446–467

CONCLUSION

A visual object is a momentary nexus of meaning binding a set of visual features from the outside world together with stuff we already know. Perhaps 95 percent of what we "see" from the outside world is already in our heads. Recognizing an object can cause both physical and cognitive action patterns to be primed facilitating future neural activation sequences. This means that seeing an object biases our brain toward a particular thought and action patterns, making them more likely.

The name psychologists give to the temporary activation of visual objects is visual working memory, and visual working memory has a capacity of between one and three chunks depending on their complexity, and these are connected to nexii of meaning. The limit of roughly three is one of the main bottlenecks in the visual thinking process. A similar number can be held in verbal working memory and often the two kinds of objects are bound together. Some objects are constructed and held only for the duration of a single fixation. A few objects are held from fixation to fixation but retaining objects reduces what can be picked up in the next fixation.

Visual working memory capacity is something that critically influences how well a design works. When we are thinking with the aid of a graphic image we are constantly picking up a chunk of information, holding it in working memory, formulating queries, and then relating what is held to a new information chunk coming in from the display. This means that the navigation costs discussed in the previous chapter are critical. For example, suppose a visual comparison is required between two graphic objects; they might be faces, pictures of houses, or diagrams. We will be much better off having them simultaneously on the same page or screen than having them on different pages. In each case visual working memory capacity is the same, but we can pick up a chunk or two, then navigate to a new point of comparison at least ten times faster with eye movements than we can switch pages (either web pages or book pages), so side-by-side comparison can be hugely more efficient.

In this chapter, we have begun to discuss the separation of visual and verbal processing in the brain. This is a good point to comment on a commonly held misconception. There is a widely held belief that there are right-brain people who are more visually creative and left-brain people who are more verbal and analytic. The actual evidence is far more complex. There is indeed some lateral specialization in the brain. Language functions tend to be concentrated on the left hand side of the brain, especially in men. Rapid processing of the locations of objects in space tends to be done more on the right. But the available evidence suggests that creativity comes as a result of the interaction between the many subsystems of the brain.[*] If there is a location for creativity it is in the frontal lobes of the brain, which provide the highest level of control over these subsystems.

[*]For a thorough review of the evidence, see Joseph B. Hellige's 1993 book, *Hemispheric Asymmetry: What's Right and What's Left* from Harvard University Press.

Chapter 7

Visual and Verbal Narrative

Forget about that old cliché, "A picture is worth a thousand words." Try to express the following in pictures.

> *If halibut is more than ten euros a kilo at Good Food, go to the fish market on 5th Street.*

It is unlikely that it could be done, even if you are capable of drawing a halibut. Good design is not about pictures versus words. The real issues are as follows: When are images most effective? When are words and other formal symbols most effective? If both images and words are used, how should they be combined?

We begin this discussion by considering sign languages used by deaf people. It may seem strange that sign languages have much to tell us about the fundamental nature of language, but thinking about them enables us to make clear distinctions about what is best expressed though words and images and diagrams. Sign language also gives us an

Visual Thinking for Information Design. DOI: https://doi.org/10.1016/B978-0-12-823567-6.00007-0

incontestable example of something that actually *is* a visual language, so we know what one looks like.

It is easy to assume that sign languages were invented by hearing people as ways of translating spoken languages, like English and French, into something the deaf could easily understand. In fact, nothing could be further from the truth. Sign languages were invented by deaf people. Mostly they arose spontaneously in the nineteenth century when previously isolated deaf children came together in schools that were created by philanthropists. Sign languages were developed by the students in those schools, not the teachers. Indeed, up until the 1980s many schools for the deaf actually prohibited signing because they believed that lip reading would better help integrate the pupils into society at large. The attempt to suppress sign language was the cause of considerable suffering since signing provides the deaf with a means of expression comparable in richness and expressive power to spoken language.◆

◆In his book on the history of sign language in America, Douglas Baynton describes how signing was banned in schools for the deaf in favor of speaking and lip reading, using techniques pioneered by Alexander Graham Bell. See *Forbidden Signs: American Culture and the Campaign Against Sign Language*. University of Chicago Press. 1996.

Sign languages are not translations of spoken languages. They are distinct languages with their own grammar and vocabularies. American Sign Language (ASL) is quite distinct from British Sign Language (BSL) and neither has the grammar of spoken English. New sign languages are still being born. In Nicaragua, linguists have watched, fascinated, as a new sign language has emerged over the past 30 years. This began to develop with the establishment of a center for special education in 1977. It has rapidly developed its own grammatical rules, demonstrating, among other things, that language is an innate capability of humans.◆

◆For more on sign languages, read Karen Emmorey's *Language, Cognition, and the Brain: Insights from Sign Language Research*, Mahwah, N.J: Erlbaum, 2002.

Although sign languages are gestural and not verbal, there are great similarities between the two forms. Both sign language and spoken language have a critical period of development. If children are not provided with the social environment for their language skills to develop in the first few years of life they will never develop fluency. Children who have grown up with animals, *enfants sauvage*, never develop language fluency because the critical period is missed.

The parts of the brain used in the understanding and production of sign languages are the same areas used in verbal language listening and talking namely, Wernicke's area and Broca's area, respectively. Sign language uses the neural subsystems normally associated with verbal processing, even though signs must pass through the visual pattern-finding machinery of the brain to get to these areas.

VISUAL THINKING VERSUS LANGUAGE-BASED THINKING

We need a clear way of distinguishing between the *visual thinking* that goes with graphic expression, and other forms of thinking, especially *language-based thinking.* The existence of sign languages clearly demolishes the idea that one mode is fundamentally visual and the other mode is fundamentally auditory. A more basic distinction between the modes of expression has to do with symbolization and logic. We shall consider these in turn.

LEARNED SYMBOLS

First and foremost, language is a socially developed system of shared symbols, together with a grammar. It can be expressed through speech, or written down or it can be signed. Natural language contains a set of nouns that denote concrete or abstract objects. These were invented. At some time in the past, a group of individuals came to a common understanding that the vocalization "dog" denoted a class of animals. Once the word was established, new individuals outside the initial group learned the symbol. For the most part these symbols accord to the *principle of arbitrariness.* There is nothing about the word dog that is dog-like. We could just as easily use the word "zab" or "cat"; the important point is that we be consistent.

Sign language signs also adhere to the principle of arbitrariness for the most part. Some gestures bear similarities to the actions they represent, especially those relating to actions, but most signs do not. Also, as a sign language becomes more sophisticated the proportion of arbitrary signs is increased.

The basis of visual thinking is pattern perception, not learned symbols. Our understanding of meaning through patterns does not come from social convention. Our perceptual machinery comes partly from evolution and partly from our visual experiences as we interact with the world; in other words, our pattern perception is partly innate and partly learned. When we see designed graphical patterns, objects and connections are perceived using this combination of perceptual processes. Patterns convey meaning in many ways that are not arbitrary and not socially determined.

Visual designs are almost always hybrids; they have aspects that support visual thinking through pattern finding, and they have aspects that are conventional and processed through the language system. Some visual symbols, for example ♥ ♪ €, are the same as words in the sense that they are agreed-on arbitrary symbols and they bear little or no resemblance to the things they represent. Actual hearts are not shaped like the symbols on valentine cards. Some realist paintings are almost entirely visual and pattern based, they do not rely on arbitrary visual symbols. Diagrams are firmly in the middle, combining meaning from agreed-on arbitrary symbols and meaning from the patterns used to show relationships.

The series of positions from the phrase "good morning" in American Sign Language. The actual sign is not a series of poses, however, but a gesture that is fluid and dynamic. This sign accords with the principle of arbitrariness; that is, there is no actual resemblance between the sign and a good morning.

www.lifeprint.com

GRAMMAR AND LOGIC

Natural language, whether it is sign language or spoken language, incorporates a form of logic that is quite distinct from the logic of visual representation. Natural language is full of qualifiers such as "if," "and," "but," "otherwise," "nevertheless," and "while." This is not formal mathematical logic, but it does allow for a kind of abstract reasoning. Such terms enable us to give conditional instructions to people, such as the directions to buy halibut with which we started this chapter. The most widely used computer programming languages are based on natural language. Statements beginning with "while," "if," and "else" provide their basic structure and this is why entry-level programming is easy to learn.

There have been many attempts to make graphical computer programming language alternatives to written languages. These have mostly failed, sometimes spectacularly. In the 1980s, a diagramming technique called the flowchart was mandated for large commercial software projects. It used symbols to express programming logic for "if" and "while" statements. An alternative technique called pseudocode has proven to be a much better way of expressing computer code in a more readable form. Pseudocode provides an explicit bridge between natural language and computer code; in pseudocode "if" and "while" statements are used much in the same way as they are in natural language. The following program counts how many large eggs and small eggs there are in a batch. It is shown using both a flowchart and pseudocode to illustrate the differences.

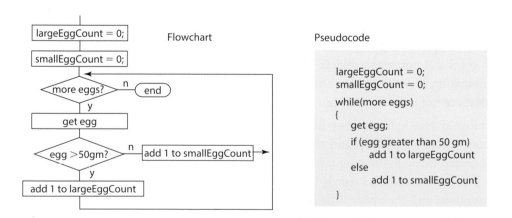

Notice that although the flowchart is called a visual language it contains almost as many words as the pseudocode. The critical difference is that the diamond shape symbols are used to represent program logic in the flowchart, whereas pseudocode uses a form similar to the natural language sentence, "If an egg is greater than 50 gm then add 1 to the large egg count, otherwise add 1 to the small egg count."

Flowcharts were a very expensive mistake. Hundreds of thousands of dollars were spent documenting computer programs in this way, only for the results to languish on shelves never to be consulted. It turned out that it was easier to read a pseudocode description, or even the program logic itself, than the flowchart. Flowcharts now stand as a reminder of the limitations of visual representation. There are some things that words do much better.

Visual representations can incorporate a kind of logic, but it is very different from the more abstract logic of natural language. Visual logic is the logic of pattern, object, and space that was discussed in Chapters 3, 5, and 6.

COMPARING AND CONTRASTING THE VERBAL AND WRITTEN MODES

Let us summarize and compare the relative strengths of verbal and visual media. Verbal, sign, and written languages provide socially designed tools for communication. The symbols and grammar are shared by hundreds of millions of people in the case of the most common languages which enormously enhances their value. Verbal, sign, and written languages use the same specialized areas of the brain for processing this information. What many people refer to as "thought," the kind of inner dialogue whereby people plan for the future and rehearse conversations with others, is mostly a form of internalized speech, sometimes called *mentalese*. This internalized language form shares the kind of rough and ready logic that comes from specialized conditional operators such as "if," "and," "but," "maybe," and "perhaps." These enable people to reason about consequences of action in ways that are very flexible.

Visual representations of information are processed by the visual system. This is an extremely powerful pattern-finding system, which is good at finding meaningful structure in diagrams. Its logic is very different than verbal logic and consists mostly of structural relationships, such as those shown on the following page. As the diagram shows, the graphic expressions of the various kinds of structural relationship work well when radically simplified and each has a corresponding verbal expression, so it cannot be claimed that this form of expression is uniquely graphic. Nevertheless, when multiple relations are combined in a diagram the graphical form can be far more succinct and easier to reason with.

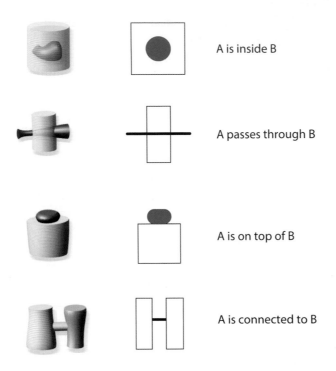

A is inside B

A passes through B

A is on top of B

A is connected to B

Almost all graphic designs are hybrids of the visual and language modes of expression and the amount of each should depend on what is to be conveyed. Words, images, and spatial patterns should be used for what they express best. In most cases images do not make good labels, and describing complex patterns of relationships with words is confusing. In the following example the structure of a small company is described in two ways, by diagram and by words. Both contain roughly the same information.

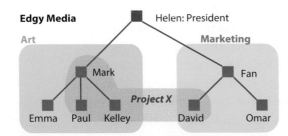

Helen is the president of the Edgy Media Company. Mark, Emma, Paul, and Kelley work in the Art department. Mark is manager of the Art department. Fan, David, and Omar work in Marketing. Fan is manager of the Marketing department. Mark, Paul, Kelly, and David are all working on Project X.

It is difficult to get an overall understanding of the Edgy Media company structure from the verbal description, but with the diagram a number of structural relationships become immediately evident; for example, that the company personnel structure is a three-level hierarchy. It is also much easier to carry out simple reasoning tasks with the aid of the diagram. Questions such as: "Who is the most senior person working on Project X?", "Which department has the most people working on Project X?", and "Who does Fan report to?" can all be addressed with simple visual queries.

LINKING WORDS AND IMAGES THROUGH DEIXIS

Even before she can speak, an infant can communicate by pointing. A reaching gesture can be interpreted as "give me that." Add some facial expression, indicating interest or dislike, and the gesture becomes modified, "that scares me" or "what is that?"

Later in life, pointing is still an important part of communication, especially when it is necessary to link visual and verbal information. Phrases like "look at that one," "put it over there," and "it's here" gain their meaning through the linking of objects to speech by gestures such as pointing. Actions that provide the subject or object of a spoken sentence by directing attention to objects in the world are called *deictic gestures.*

Richard Bolt of the MIT media lab captured this concept succinctly with the phrase "put that there."[*] This phase is uttered with two pointing gestures. The first denotes the object to be moved and the second denotes the intended location. What is special about this sentence is that the words "that" and "there" only gain their referents by being combined with pointing.

*R.A. Bolt, 1980. Put-that-there: Voice and gesture at the graphics interface. *Proceedings of the 7th Annual Conference on Computer Graphics and interactive Techniques. SIGGRAPH.* 262–270.

Deictic gestures can be accomplished in many more ways than pointing with a finger. The direction of someone's gaze, or how he orients his body, can also serve to denote the subject of an utterance.

Get it away from me!

All this can be yours!!

Deictic gestures can have more elaborate semantics than simple designation of an object. A large circular gesture can indicate a group of objects. The vagueness or precision of a gesture can express the degree of uncertainty in what is being denoted.

POWERPOINT PRESENTATIONS AND POINTING

In formal meetings people often stand up in front of screens, run through a set of slides, and present their ideas. A good lecture using Microsoft's PowerPoint is a combination of imagery presented on a screen and words provided by the presenter. The perceptual and cognitive theory given in this and the previous chapter suggests the following guidelines. PowerPoint slides should be primarily devoted to images and diagrams. Only essential text should be placed on the slide; for example, labels to make a diagram comprehensible and perhaps a title to set up a question that the narrator can answer. Narrative should be provided by the speaker through spoken words. Deictic gestures should link the two media. A clear deictic gesture allows the speaker to direct the visual attention of audience members to different parts of the visual imagery.

Although these points may seem quite obvious, PowerPoint slides are often poorly designed. In many cases people put far too many words on the slides, causing the viewer to read the slides, rather than listen to the presenter. Words that match what the speaker is saying can be the worst of all. People will often read ahead and then mentally wander off as the speaker catches up. It is also a common mistake for the slide to contain a set of section "bullets" listing the main points. Generally these belong in the speakers notes, not on the screen. They also have the effect of weakening narrative tension because the viewer will look ahead and reason about the conclusion bullet long before the speaker gets there.

Until recently, a major shortcoming in PowerPoint software was the lack of an effective pointer to link the words of the speaker with the

In the movie *An Inconvenient Truth*, former Vice President Al Gore uses visual imagery to powerfully convey the potential dangers of global warming. There are very few words on his slides. He is clearly illuminated so that his speech and gestures can be effective.

graphic content of the screen. This has been remedied with a simulated laser pointer and the ability to "draw" on a slide using the mouse with a result resembling the use of a highlighting marker. To realize the full value of PowerPoint presentations the use of these deictic supports, or something similar, is essential.

Gestures are an important part of communication and there should be light on the speaker so that his or her gestures are clear. Unfortunately this, too, is usually lacking. Most lecture rooms are dimmed to make the slides clear and there is no provision to illuminate the speaker.

MIRROR NEURONS: COPYCAT CELLS

In the early 1990s an Italian team of researchers, led by Giacomo Rizzolatti, made a discovery that relates to one of the most fundamental cognitive capacities we have.[*] He was carrying out a study of the motor cortex of a monkey and had inserted a tiny micro electrode into a neuron in its motor cortex. This neuron, like others in the same region of the brain, sent out electrical signals whenever the monkey reached out to move an object.

[*]G. Rizzolatti and L. Craighero, 2004. The mirror-neuron system. *Annual Review of Neuroscience.* 27: 169–192.

The experiment was proceeding much as usual when something remarkable happened. A graduate student had entered the lab eating an ice cream cone. This got the monkey's attention and when the student raised the cone to his lips, the monkey's neuron responded just as it had when it moved its own hands.

This event marked the discovery of *mirror neurons* which have since been discovered in many areas of the brain. Mirror neurons exhibit activation in the *same neural pathways* that would normally be used to execute a particular action. Thus they provide a basis for learning by imitation. They have been found in many primates, and evidence suggests that they are especially prevalent in humans. They have been called "empathy neurons" because they may allow us to read the emotions of others through the same pathways that generate our own facial expressions when we are expressing emotions.[*]

[*]According to the research by psychologist Paul Ekman, there are seven basic and universal facial expressions expressing emotion: anger, sadness, fear, surprise, disgust, contempt, and happiness. P. Ekman, 2003. *Emotions Revealed. Recognizing Faces and Feelings to Improve Communication and Emotional Life.* Times Books, New York.

Mirror neurons support a pre-language form of communication that maps action onto action. They probably provide the basis of a "gut feeling" level of empathic communication. Indeed, some scientists speculate that the mirror neuron system may be critical to the complex social structure maintained by humans. Mirror neurons support a relatively unsophisticated nonsymbolic moment-to-moment form of communication. We now turn our attention to the much more complex forms of communication that are involved in storytelling.

We may feel the emotions of others via our own facial muscles through the mediation of mirror neurons. These illustrations of anger, fear, joy, and sadness are from Gary Faigin, *The Artist's Complete Guide to Facial Expression*. Watson Guptill Publications. New York, 1990.

VISUAL NARRATIVE: CAPTURING THE COGNITIVE THREAD

To be effective, a presenter must capture the *cognitive thread* of the audience. The *cognitive thread* is the sequence of concepts that are held actively in visual and verbal working memories, together with the links between them.♦ If a movie or presentation is successful, the cognitive thread of audience members will roughly follow the narrative thread that the author has designed. This means that designing for narrative is very different than designing for information seeking.

♦We are using the term "concept" here to refer to the temporary nexus of meaning, as described in the previous chapter.

Browsing information seekers have highly individual cognitive threads which are shaped moment-to-moment by the specific demands of the cognitive process of solving a problem. This process is internally driven. Conversely, the audience of a narrative presentation will, if they are attending, have cognitive threads that are much more similar to each other, although still far from identical because of the variety of their prior experiences. A professional film critic and a regular movie fan will see many things differently in a movie, but in each frame they both will look mostly at the same visual objects in the same order and this will result in many of the same concepts being activated in the same order.

The goal of most presentations is to build or enhance *predictive mental models* in the minds of the audience. The importance of predictive models in cognition in general and presentations in particular is the subject of the next chapter. Here we are concerned with the more detailed mechanics.

The broad framework around which narratives are built has three components: establishing a problem, elaborating a problem, and resolving a problem. The kind of problem and the nature of its resolution depend on the genre. In a mystery thriller, finding a murderer is often the problem.

A lecture about science will generally have some unsolved puzzle about the nature of the world as the problem. In a business presentation, the problem may be opening up a new market for a particular type of product.

This pattern of setting up, elaborating, and resolving is repeated at many levels in a narrative. The same pattern can be found in a single short dialogue as well as longer episodes. It makes the audience seek for cognitive resolution and this provides the motivation for sustained attention. As we shall see in this chapter, narrative can be carried either visually or through verbal language.

Q&A PATTERNS

An example of short time scale visual narrative is the question and answer (Q&A) pattern used in cinematography. In his book on cinematography, Steven Katz discusses the three-shot sequence as a method for accomplishing narrative tension on a small scale. He calls these Q&A patterns. The first two shots provide seemingly unrelated information and this leads the viewer to question the connection between these ideas. The third shot then provides the link and the resolution.◆

◆Most of the points relating to cinematography come from a book by S.D. Katz, 1991. *Film Directing Shot by Shot: visualizing from concept to the screen*. Michael Weiss Productions and Focal Press.

A simple example has become a cinematic cliché. First we see a woman walking along a street toward the right side of the screen; she is carrying a pile of parcels. Because the camera follows her, our eyes follow her. Next we follow a man also walking along a street. He is moving quickly toward the left side of the screen. In the third shot, the two collide and the parcels spill on the sidewalk. This provides the resolution of the three-shot sequence, but opens up a new question: what will be the future relationship of these two people?

VISUAL FRAMING

At the most basic level the main task for the author of a visual narrative is to capture and control what the audience is looking at, and hence attending to, from moment to moment. Part of this is done simply by carefully framing each shot and by designing the transitions between shots so that intended object attention becomes inescapable. Cinematographers have worked out how to do this with great precision.

The camera frame itself is a powerful device for controlling attention. Anything outside of it cannot be visually attended and so framing a scene divides the world into the class of objects that can be attended and those that cannot. Within the frame, objects can be arranged to bias attention. Having the critical objects or people at the center of the screen, having the camera follow a moving object, or having only the critical objects in focus are all methods for increasing the likelihood that we will attend according to the cinematographer's plans.

83- SAY HELLO TO MRS. ROBINSON, BENJAMIN

84- HELLO, MRS. ROBINSON

84- HELLO BENJAMIN.

Storyboards are sketches used to plan a sequence of shots in movie making.

This is the sequence of storyboards for the movie *The Graduate* by Harold Michelson. It shows the first time that Benjamin, a recently graduated student, meets Mrs. Robinson, with whom he will later have an affair.

Because of the way the camera frames the shots, a viewer has little choice but to attend first to Benjamin's father, next to Benjamin lazing on a float in the pool and finally to Mrs. Robinson.

(From S.D. Katz, 1990. Film Directing, *Shot by Shot: Visualizing from Concept to the Screen*. Michael Weise Productions, Studio City, CA.)

Cinematographers pay great attention to the background of a shot. Anything that is visually distinctive, but irrelevant, is like an invitation to viewers to switch their attention to that item and away from the narrative thread. One mechanism for making the background less likely to attract attention is through the careful application of depth of focus. Increasing the lens aperture of a camera has the effect that only objects at a particular depth are in sharp focus. Everything that is closer or further away then becomes blurred and less likely to capture the viewer's attention.

FINSTS AND DIVIDED ATTENTION

The human eye has only one fovea and so we can only fixate one point at a time, or follow a single moving object. The brain, however, has mechanisms that allow us to keep track of several objects in the visual field, although we do not perceive much of these secondary objects. Zenon Pylyshyn, a psychologist at the University of Western Ontario in Canada, studied this capability and found that the maximum number of objects people could track was four. He called the mental markers that are placed on the moving objects FINSTs for *fin*gers of *inst*antiation.[*]

In Pylyshyn's experiments, keeping track of moving objects was all the participants had to do, but the task required intense concentration; under more normal circumstances our cognitive activity is much more varied. It is unlikely that our brains usually track more than one or two objects in addition to the one we are focally attending.

Suppose we are watching children in a crowded playground. The FINST capability means that we can maintain fixation on one child and simultaneously, in the periphery of our vision, keep track of one or two others. We do not get much information about the actions of those other children, but if we need to know about them the FINST marker means that a visual query, by means of an eye movement taking less than a tenth of a second, is all that is required to check on them.

The practical implication of FINSTs for cinematographers or video game designers is that it is possible to create a visually chaotic scene, and for the audience or player to keep track of up to four actors to some extent, even though only one can be the immediate focus of attention at any instant. More than this and they will lose track.

[*]Z.W. Pylyshyn, 1989. The role of location indexes in spatial perception: A sketch of the FINST spatial-index model. *Cognition*. 32: 65–97.

The brain can keep track of three or four moving objects at once.

SHOT TRANSITIONS

Because of saccadic eye movements, perception is punctuated; the brain processes a series of distinct images with information concentrated at the fovea. The eye fixates on a point of interest, the brain grabs the image and processes it, the eye moves rapidly and fixates on another point of interest, the brain processes that image, and so on. The low capacity of visual working memory means that only a few points of correspondence are retained from one fixation to the next. These points are only what is relevant to the task at hand, typically consisting of the locations of one or two of the objects that have been fixated recently together with information about their rough layout in space in the context of scene gist.

The fact that perception itself is a discrete, frame-by-frame process accounts for why we are so good at dealing with shot transitions in movies. Cinematographers often shift abruptly from one camera's view to another camera's view causing an abrupt jump in the image. This is a narrative device to redirect our attention within a scene or to another scene. Transitions from shot to shot must be carefully designed to avoid disorientation. The visual continuity of ideas can be as useful and effective as the verbal continuity of ideas. One common technique is the *establishing shot*, followed by the focus shot. For example, from a distance we see a character on the street, talking to another person. Then we switch to a closer image of the two people and hear their dialogue. The first establishing shot provides gist and the layout of objects that will later be the target of several focal shots. Manuals for cinematographers such as the Katz book provide detailed catalogues of various shot transitions. These can all be regarded as devices for manipulating the cognitive thread of the audience. If shot transitions are done well, most members of the audience will look at the same objects in the same sequence.

CARTOONS AND NARRATIVE DIAGRAMS

Strip cartoons are a form of visual narrative that have much in common with movies. They substitute printed words for spoken words, and they substitute a series of still images for moving pictures. Like movie shot transitions, the frames of a cartoon strip rely on the brain's ability to make sense of a series of discrete images. Although there are enormous differences in the visual style of a cartoon strip compared to a Hollywood movie, it is remarkable how similar they are cognitively.

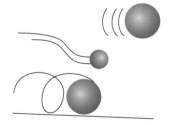

The lack of real motion in a cartoon strip frame is compensated for by the use of action lines. These are graphical strokes that show movement pathways. In one respect, action lines are arbitrary symbols; real objects do not have lines trailing them when they move. In another respect, they are not arbitrary because they explicitly show the recent history of an object, and by extrapolation, the immediate future.

Short-term prediction is one of the most important functions of the brain. In a sense, the brain is constantly making predictions about the state of the world that will follow from actions such as eye or hand movements. When the state of the world is not as expected, neural alarm bells go off or, in the words of computer science, exceptions are triggered.* This short-term prediction can be thought of in terms of pattern processing. The patterns that are picked up at various levels of the visual system have a temporal dimension as well as a spatial dimension. Once a temporal pattern is detected by a set of neurons, the abrupt cessation of that pattern will trigger an exception. For example, one of the most

*In his book, *On Intelligence* (Time Books, 2004), Jeff Hawkins argues that prediction is a fundamental operation found universally in brain structures. When temporal patterns fail to play out, special *exception* signals are triggered to be handled by higher-level processing units.

basic temporal patterns is the assumption of object persistence discussed in the previous chapter. When an object marked by a FINST disappears, an exception is triggered and a shift of attention will likely ensue. It is remarkable that the simple forms of cartoon action lines can capture and express this basic function; the ball seen in the static illustrations shown here is projected forwards in time, like a ball that we see in the real world. In a subsequent frame we would expect these moving objects to continue their motion paths.

MIXED MODE VISUALIZATION NARRATIVES

With the advent of the Internet and online pedagogy, there are many modes of narrative where control over the cognitive thread is mixed; it switches back and forth, sometimes the presentation is in control, sometimes the learner is in control.

A common form of mixed mode visualization is the interactive web story with drill down options. In this form, a main narrative thread containing visualization images and supporting text contains links at various points where more depth and detail optionally can be obtained. The main thread may be either a set of individual pages, like a slide show, or a long scrollable page, as is commonly used in blogs. Both forms enable the person to either read the text and view the images sequentially, essentially ceding their cognitive thread to the presentation, or they can jump back and forth in the sequence, and drill down, taking more control over their own cognitive processes.◆

◆Edward Segel and Jeffrey Heer (2010) elucidate a number of categories of mixed mode forms of visualization in "Narrative visualization: Telling stories with data." IEEE *Transactions on Visualization and Computer Graphics.* 16(6): 1139–1148.

The obvious advantages in this form of presentation is that many people in a target audience will already know much of what is being presented, and they can therefore focus their attention mostly on the parts they do not know.

SINGLE-FRAME NARRATIVES

Some single-frame diagrams are designed to perform a narrative function; they lead the interpreter through a series of cognitive steps in a particular order. One example is given on the following page in the form of a poster designed by R.G. Franklin and R.J.W. Turner. Its goals are to educate the public on the way water is used in a modern house and to encourage conservation.

The narrative thread in this diagram is less demanding than in the multiframe cartoon strip; nevertheless, the intention that the ideas be explored in a particular order is expressed by the sequence of arrows connecting the different major components.

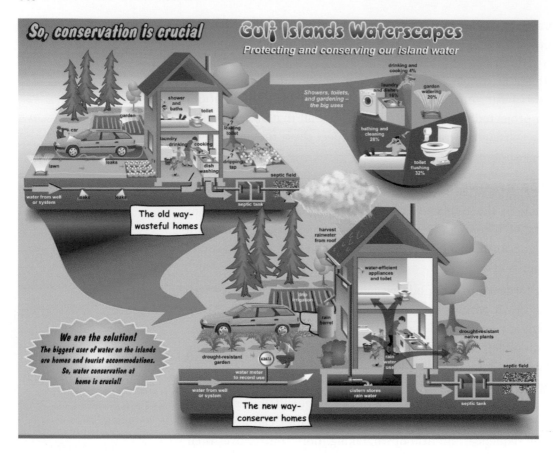

CONCLUSION

We began this chapter by discussing the fundamental differences between visual and linguistic forms of expression. Linguistic forms of expression are characterized by the use of a rich set of socially invented arbitrary symbols as well as a form of logic exemplified by the "ifs," "ands," and "buts" of natural language. The grammar of visual representation is quite different having to do with pattern relationships such as "connected to," "inside," "outside," or "part of." This means that certain kinds of logic are best left to verbal or written language.

Narrative, however, can be carried either through language or purely visual techniques or both. This is because narrative is about leading the attention of an audience and this can be achieved through either modality, although what can be expressed within a narrative is very different depending on which one is used. Language can convey complex logical relationships between abstract ideas and support conditional actions. Visual media can support the perception of almost instantaneous scene gist, rapid explorations of spatial structure and relationships between objects, as well as emotions and motivations. Both can maintain and hold the thread of audience attention which is the essence of narrative.

One of the first choices to be made when designing a visual communication is the desired strength of the narrative form. Movies and animated cartoons are the strongest visual narrative forms because they exert the most control over serial attention to visual objects and actions. Graphic cartoons can also provide narrative but exert an intermediate-level control over the cognitive thread; cartoon frames are intended to be perceived in a particular order but allow for random access. Diagrams of various kinds as well as pictures and photographs are capable of conveying some sense of narrative, although this is less than movies and cartoon strips. Usually the viewer must actively discover the narrative in a diagram of still image, unlike the inescapable narrative train of a movie.

Chapter 8

Building Mental Models: Why We Present with Visualizations

Suppose you are making a presentation about the loss of animal habitat in the environment, complete with pictures of animals, maps showing the distributions of plants and animals, and charts showing how the number of birds, bugs, mammals, and fish have declined over the last 30 years. Why are you doing it? There are many possible answers. Presumably you want your audience to remember what you are saying and to remember the information in the images on your slides. You probably want them to learn something about the environment. Ultimately, if your presentation is to be truly effective, you hope that people will change their behavior in some way as a result of what you have shown them. The change in behavior might have many forms, from greater support for conservation measures to the direct application of the methodologies or theories you have presented. But it is action that counts.

Visual Thinking for Information Design. DOI: https://doi.org/10.1016/B978-0-12-823567-6.00008-2

This chapter introduces a radical new theory about the function and purpose of the brain. The theory explains how presentations can change behaviors by altering *executable mental models*. It provides reasons for using particular types of visualization and illuminates how each can contribute to mental model development.

We will refer to this theory generically as *predictive cognition*.[*] It is an all-encompassing theory about what cognition is for, what memory is for, and what communication is about. As we shall see, it upends many traditional views. Here we will use it to provide a new basis for thinking about the kinds of visualization that are best used in presentations and their functional roles in mental model construction.

According to the *predictive cognition* theory, the fundamental purpose "guiding" the architecture and activities of the brain is predicting the future. It is often assumed that predicting the future is impossible, and indeed this is true for such things as predicting the value of the stock market in a year's time, or the prime minister of a country in 10 years. But in fact our brains predict the future all the time, from moment to moment, from day to day, and for longer terms. We could not function otherwise. At the most basic short-term level, our brains predict the results of eye movements and hand movements. An action, such as a hand movement, is planned in the motor cortex, and at the same time the consequences of that hand movement are simulated. The brain simulation predicts that the hand will come into contact with the object to be grasped and that it will get a neural confirmation from touch sensors in the fingertips. The neural action plan is executed, the hand moves, and the fingers come into contact with the surface; sensory confirmation is received. But sometimes, something goes wrong. Perhaps the object was moved, or our hand movement may have been clumsy. Whatever the case, an exception is triggered, and the mismatch between the predicted consequence and actual consequences causes higher-level brain processes to come into play to address the situation. This is a very efficient way of organizing the brain because most of the time everything goes as planned and higher-level functions of the brain are not required to control lower-level actions, like grasping, walking, or forming words.

When we are driving we are continuously making unconscious predictions about how other vehicles and our own car will behave (e.g. stay in lanes). Our brains are running an ongoing predictive model, which incorporates the normal behaviors of vehicles, generally staying in lanes, maintaining speed and responding as usual to acceleration and steering. We can thereby drive with minimal cognitive attention

[*]An excellent introduction to the theory of predictive cognition can be found in A. Clark, 2013. Whatever next? Predictive brains, situated agents, and the future of cognitive science. *Behavioral and Brain Sciences*. 36(3): 181–204.

and are free to daydream or plan our day. But if something unusual occurs—a car in front veers out of its lane—an exception is triggered and the lower-level brain mechanisms send a request for help from higher-level processes. The situation comes to our conscious attention, engaging higher responses. It will also interrupt our daydreaming or day planning.

EPISODIC MEMORY

As the term suggests, *episodic memory* is how we recall episodes in the form of events that unfold in space and time.[*] It is evident that episodic memory, unlike declarative memory (of facts), is a constructive process; it is not a simple replay. Predictive cognition theory proposes that episodic memories are based on a process of *scenario construction*; our brains construct a running *simulation* of what might have happened based partly on what we specifically recall, but mostly on our general purpose mental models of the world and how it operates. In other words, high-level memory consists of an *executable simulation of possible events that occurred in the past.*

[*]E. Tulving, 1972. Episodic and semantic memory. *Organization of Memory*. 1: 381–403.

The predictive cognition theory goes further. It holds that predicting the future and remembering the past are essentially the same process. In both cases, we start with a small amount of knowledge regarding the state of the world and run a simulation to construct or reconstruct events using general-purpose predictive models of how the world functions. The only real difference is the starting point.

Furthermore, remembering the past is really a *secondary* function of a basic cognitive capacity, which underlies many capabilities including navigation, future planning, and imagination, as well as episodic memory. Among other things, this explains why memory in general is so poor. Most people cannot, for example, remember what they ate for lunch 2 weeks previously.

Why do we need to remember at all? Logically, it should not be necessary. Our continued success depends on our actions now and in the future, not on what we did in the past. According to Johannes Mahr and Gergely Csibra, two psychologists working in Hungary, the reason for our remembering the past is specifically so that we can construct stories and communicate our executable mental models to others.[*] In their view, as language capacity evolved, the episodic memory system evolved to support it. Moreover, a major purpose of language is for individuals to transmit information via speech, enabling others to refine their executable mental models of the world.

[*]J.B. Mahr and G. Csibra, 2015. Why do we remember? The communicative function of episodic memory. *Behavioral and Brain Sciences*. 41, 1–63.

It is thought that most of the cognitive functions unique to humans developed between 50,000 and 150,000 years ago, a very long period when humans were in the hunter-gatherer stage (the more recent period of recorded history is too short for significant evolution). According to this hypothesis, during the hunter-gatherer period speech developed to support the transmission of mental models regarding survival techniques. Language enabled groups of early humans to communicate executable mental models supporting how and where to hunt or find edible plants.

There are interesting parallels with lessons learned by researchers working in artificial intelligence (AI) and robotics. For decades, the main focus of AI was planning either the next move or the next series of moves. Now that robots and AI are finally becoming successful, researchers have come to realize that predictive planning is not enough. Sometimes we need a robot to tell us why it acted in a certain way. As with humans, planning by simulating the future is primary, the explanation is secondary, but it is nevertheless important to communicate the reasons for actions; in other words, robots must communicate their mental models to their handlers.

LONG-TERM MEMORY

When we look at something, perhaps 95 percent of what we consciously perceive is not what is "out there" but what is already in our heads in long-term memory. The reason we have the impression of perceiving a rich and complex environment is that we have rich and complex networks of meaning stored in our brains. This meaning becomes activated by the quite small amount of information that actually makes it through the visual processing system to visual working memory. This is why many husbands do not notice when their wives have new hairstyles and wives do not notice when their husbands shave off beards or moustaches. What is perceived of our wives and husbands is mostly what we have previously learned about them.

Long-term memory should not be thought of as a separate storage area in the brain, like a computer disc drive, where information is dumped after it has been processed by the sensory systems. It is not a distinct unit; rather the brain is a system where every neuron both processes and stores information. V4 processes and stores visual pattern information; as we learn to identify new patterns, neural circuits are formed and strengthened to process those patterns. Similarly, the inferotemporal cortex both processes and stores higher-level cognitive sequencing operations that relate, for example, to the sequence of steps we carry out when performing a visual task, such as reading a map. Long-term memories are the executable mental models we have been discussing.

The processes of visual thinking make up a particular class of executable memories. These are very diverse, because what we think about is very diverse. Most visual thinking involves situated interactions with the environment. Consider for a moment the following three examples: reading a statistical bar chart, merging onto an expressway in an automobile, and discussing a project in a face-to-face meeting. These seem very different, but each requires the interpretation of visual information and a structured sequence of actions depending on the information. Each is a skilled activity involving patterns of cognitive action that are refined and consolidated every time we perform the act successfully. They are also improved when mistakes are made, recognized, and corrected. Visual-thinking procedures apply memory patterns that have been stored as action sequences. This is what constitutes the skill of visual thinking.

A midbrain structure, the hippocampus, is key to the formation of long-term memories. The evidence for this is striking; some unfortunate people have had their hippocampi damaged on both sides of the brain, and as a result they are completely unable to consolidate memories of events that happened after the damage occurred. These people will greet their relatives as if there had been a long absence, even if they have been out of the room for only a few minutes. The hippocampus is also critical to spatial planning, containing a representation of where we are with respect to other objects in our immediate vicinity. It is critical in handling the spatial aspects of cognitive simulations.

For executable memories to develop, there must be either an internal or external consequence associated with a cognitive act. Interpreting a bar chart and coming to a useful conclusion, perhaps about a business strategy, will yield an internal cognitive reward and similarly enhance the neural patterns that occurred during the interpretation. An external consequence might be that a particular sequence of neural processes leads to a solution to a problem. For example, making it onto the freeway smoothly will enhance and consolidate the neural patterns that lead to the particular sequence of eye movements, head movements, visual processing of the pattern of moving vehicles, and steering movements that yielded the successful outcome. A successful dialogue with a co-worker, involving visually interpreting facial expressions, may yield an external social reward in the form of a smile. In each case, the reward strengthens the pathways supporting a neural activation sequence that underlies the processing of information. The long-term memory that is gained supports particular cognitive action sequences and so skill is acquired. Long-term memory results from a strengthening of neural connections, increasing the likelihood that a particular neural chain reaction will occur.

PRIMING

To illustrate a point in a presentation, I might look through a few hundred images in a database. But little is retained for explicit memory access; next day it is likely that I will be unable to explicitly recall having seen more than two or three. Nevertheless, some trace of the others remains in my brain. If I need to revisit the same database to find a new image, I will be able to skim through the images quite a bit faster. Somehow I can rule out all of the irrelevant images faster because I have seen them recently. This effect is called long-term priming, or *perceptual facilitation*, and it is a form of implicit memory. Any images that we see, and process to some extent, prime the visual pathways involved in their processing. This means that those images, and similar images, will be processed faster the second time around. Repeat processing is easier, at least for a day or two.

Priming is the reason artists and designers often prepare for a particular creative bout by reviewing relevant images and other materials for a day or two. This gets the relevant circuits into a primed state. When long-term memories are reactivated we become primed for action. Or in other words, a particular set of simulations are brought to a state of partial readiness.

PREDICTIVE COGNITION AND PRESENTATIONS

Having introduced the predictive cognition theory, we now turn our attention to what it can tell us about making visualizations for the purpose of presentation. Perhaps none of the guidelines we can derive are entirely new, but the theory gives them more focus and depth. A frequent admonition to public speakers is that they should know their audience. Predictive cognition translates this into the much more analytic.

Know and understand your audience's mental models and how they may be adapted and extended.

In terms of visualization, this guidance has many levels of meaning. At the most basic, it means: does your audience understand how to think with the particular kind of chart you are using? If not, tell them how it works. Even common charts, such as time series plots, need their axes explained. The inventors of creative and innovative visualizations frequently think their designs are as transparent and understandable to the audience as they are to themselves. This is usually not the case and even with the best innovations the presenter must spend a sufficient amount of time explaining how the different components of the visualization convey meaning. A presenter using a new kind of visualization runs the risk that more cognitive effort will be devoted to understanding it than understanding what it represents. Most of the time, the medium should not dominate the message. This is why sticking to conventional maps, bar charts, and node link diagrams is usually preferred.

At a higher cognitive level, it is necessary to have an understanding of the common mental models likely to be held by the audience in the subject area. Naturally, these can be hugely diverse, reflecting the diversity of human knowledge. In general, it is best to aim the presentation somewhere below the median level of understanding. But the goal has to be to develop a framework of existing mental models within which whatever is new can be assimilated. To maintain and hold attention, a presenter should build links between the subject matter and issues of broader importance. Most technical detail can usually be omitted, except where it is central, assuming of course that the audience has access to more detail at a later date. Usually, the most important thing is for people to understand how what they are being offered may be useful, and ideally to be convinced that further investigation will be worthwhile.

Other guidelines are less straightforward. For example, research from the field of linguistics suggests that people are more likely to understand stories about data and assimilate them into their mental models, if they are couched in terms of *animate agents*. Goldin-Meadow has hypothesized that an agent-patient-act order may be the natural way of comprehending events.[•] In this rather technical language from the field of linguistics, the "agent" is something that could be a person, an animal, or even an inanimate agent of change, whereas the "patient" is what is acted on—the target of an action. In other words, cause and effect are built into our mental models–mediated active agents.

[•]S. Goldin-Meadow, W.C. So, A. Özyürek, and C. Mylander, 2008. The natural order of events: How speakers of different languages represent events nonverbally. *Proceedings of the National Academy of Sciences*. 105(27): 9163–9168.

Certainly there is abundant evidence that agent-based thinking provides the underpinnings of much of human cognition, along with visual spatial metaphors.[•] Because of this early development, predictive mental models are not pure abstractions, instead they work through deep metaphors that underlie all cognition. So, arguably, visualizations will be more readily understood if they incorporate active agents as metaphors.

[•]Steven Pinker's book *The Stuff of Thought* (2007) is about verbal language, but it is striking how much of it is based on visual spatial metaphors. Published by Penguin.

ANALYZING SEAWEED AND BUILDING MENTAL MODELS

I am going to use an extended example from my own work to illustrate some of the ways that visualizations can support mental model building.

In the fall of 2014 I had a conversation with biologist and ecologist, Dr. Jenn Dijkstra, which began a consuming research collaboration. One of her main interests is the seaweeds that cover the seafloor in the shallower parts of the oceans and the many little creatures that live in the spaces between the seaweed branches. These spaces provide refuge from predation by small fish. Describing such predator-prey relationships is fundamental to understanding how species, both plants and animals, depend on one another in the environment. Together, Dijkstra and I developed a new way of describing the spatial structure of seaweeds, particularly the space within seaweed fronds that can help us understand predator-prey relationships.

To illustrate some of the ways different kinds of visualization can contribute to mental model building, I am going to use examples from the way we have presented this work and tell two stories in parallel. One is the story of seaweeds and the method we developed for describing their spatial structures. The second is an analysis of how each of the visualizations we use to present the results is designed to build and enrich predictive mental models. We have each made a number of presentations of this work, and the following examples are drawn from those presentations.

Specifically, in terms of mental model development we have the following goals for our presentations. We hope that our audience will, through the presentation: (1) form or elaborate a mental model about the seaweeds that grow on the seabed and form the habitat for many small organisms; (2) form or elaborate a mental model of sweeping changes that have occurred in the seaweed environment in the Gulf of Maine, off the north-eastern coast of the United States; (3) form or elaborate a mental model of how seaweed provides refuge for small animals from predation by larger animals; and (4) form a mental model of how our new method can be used in describing the spatial architecture of different seaweeds, and how it may be used to enhance understanding of ecologically important interactions within these habitats.

PHOTOGRAPHS

We begin our presentations with photographic images. Although words are usually the clearest and most succinct way of making a point, they may not have much impact on their own. It is easy to make statements like: "The distribution of seaweed in the Gulf of Maine has changed radically over the past few years. There has been an invasion of a seaweed called *Dasysiphonia japonica*." These two declarative sentences may indeed capture what we are hoping to convey. But the words by themselves are unlikely to have much impact on anyone's executable mental model.

Photographic images have an incomparable ability to enrich mental models and thereby make presentations more memorable.

  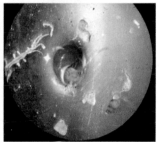

The image on the left shows a section of seafloor covered with invasive seaweed. Even though most of the image is filled with the reddish invader, a forlorn blade of kelp is a reminder of the kind of seaweed that used to dominate the seafloor. A diver is taking a sample with a plastic bag. Even the most rational scientist responds to human presence. Having the diver taking samples in the photograph is valuable in a number of ways. It adds to the mental model of how this research must be carried out; a diver must collect samples of seaweed in a plastic bag. The image also conveys something of the difficulty of doing field research in such a complex environment. The image on the right shows a single sample of invasive seaweed to give a better idea of its structure (technically these are not plants but a form of algae). On the lower right is a microscope image to provide a mental model of the kinds of inhabitants living within the seaweed fronds.

CARTOONS TO SUPPORT MENTAL MODEL BUILDING

It is commonly understood that the main reason for little critters to live in seaweeds is to be safe from small fish that would love to eat them.

Seaweeds provide places of refuge from larger predators. The fronds of a seaweed provide a physical barrier through which the little animals can pass but which block larger animals. Some scientists use the term *spatial sieve* to describe this function. This provides a mental model based on a physical device that separates items of different sizes. Small items can pass through a sieve, large items cannot.

We use a simple cartoon showing a hungry fish, a simple mesh sieve, and a few small creatures to enhance this mental model.

MECHANICAL MODELS USING ANIMATION

Dijkstra and I developed a method for describing the architecture of the spaces between seaweed fronds (called interstitial spaces), which we called *spherical space analysis*. Because it is impossible to simulate how all the different shapes and sizes of animals can wriggle into the branches of a seaweed, we decided to simplify and consider only idealized spherical organisms. The goal is to estimate the *volume of refuge* there is within the branches of a seaweed for an idealized prey organism to escape from another larger predatory organism.

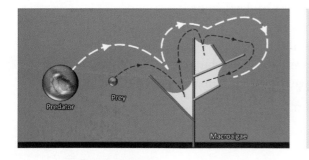

Drew Stevens, one of the graduate students involved in the project, came up with a simple Microsoft PowerPoint animation to illustrate the concept. The predator is animated along the dashed lines, and at each inflexion point a yellow area appears to illustrate areas it cannot reach. The prey subsequently is animated along a path entering each of the areas of refuge.

Of course, our goal as scientists is that other scientists will adopt this way of interpreting the architectural space of seaweeds. In other words, they will incorporate spherical space analysis into the set of mental models, whereby they understand predator-prey relationships. Ultimately, we hope they will adopt this method and apply it to other environments, such as small birds in bushes sheltering from predatory hawks.

In a follow-up visualization, we transition from the cartoonish to the technical and use the following image to show how volume of refuge varies with different sizes of spherical organisms for a particular seaweed example—in this case another invasive species called *Codium fragile*. This visualization was developed by William Ikedo, another student involved in the project. The yellow areas represent volumes inaccessible to idealized organisms of different sizes.

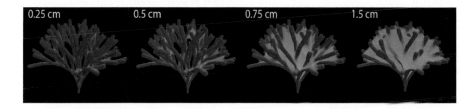

CHARTS AND GRAPHS

Charts and graphs may seem to be the most visually uninteresting part of a presentation. They always need careful explanation with the mental model in mind.

In academic papers, complex charts like the one shown on the following page are common. Arguably, they should not be given in a presentation where only a minute or two is available to explain them. We take the opposite position and show this figure in all its complexity; however, we highlight only the most striking numbers, the two points indicated with arrows. These show that there are approximately 30,000 small animals in a square meter of seafloor covered in invasive *Dasysiphonia*, whereas there are only about 100 in a square meter of the kelp. This very dramatic finding implies that there are far more little critters on the sea floor off the coast of New England than there used to be. And this is a consequence of the seaweed invader. Also, this astonishingly large difference is predicted by the difference in inaccessible volumes computed by our method.

But why show the rest of the points on the chart if they are not going to be discussed? We could use a simplified chart with only two points on it. The answer is that we want the audience to have in their mental models that there is much more information and depth of understanding to be gained by reading the research paper.

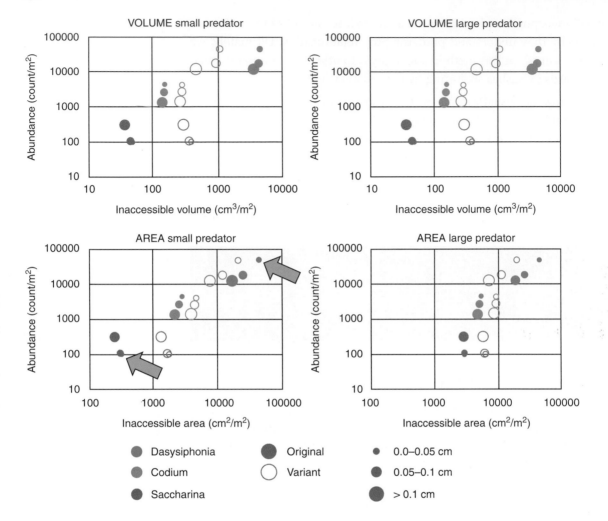

We do not know the broader implications of a population explosion of small creatures. What we have done is add a cognitive tool to understand ecological interactions within the context of seafloor habitat. Visualizations are an essential part of how we explain this tool.

We now turn our attention to what predictive cognition can say about other kinds of visualizations.

NARRATIVE ASSEMBLY DIAGRAMS

Some visual narratives are designed explicitly for the communication of executable mental models. Assembly diagrams are an example. Certain products like shelving and playground toys often come disassembled. Assembly instructions have the classic form of a narrative, in that a problem is posed (assembling something), elaborated (the detailed steps), and hopefully resolved (the fully assembled object). Executing the mental model results in a piece of furniture coming into being.

A group of researchers at Stanford University led by Barbara Tversky studied the cognitive process involved in following assembly instructions.[*] They measured how successful people were at assembling furniture using a variety of diagrammatic instruction styles. As the result of a series of such studies, they developed a set of cognitive principles for assembly instructions together with exemplary sequences of diagrams. The main principles were as follows.

[*]J. Heiser, D. Phan, M. Agrawala, B. Tversky, and P. Hanrahan, 2004. Identification and validation of cognitive design principles for automated generation of assembly instructions. Proceedings of *Advanced Visual Interfaces*. 311–319.

- **A clear sequence of operations should be evident to maintain the narrative sequence**. This might be accomplished with a cartoon-like series of frames, each showing a major step in the assembly.
- **Components should be clearly visible and identifiable in the diagrams**. This is largely a matter of clear illustration. It is important to choose a viewpoint from which all components are visible. With more complex objects a transparent representation of some components may help accomplish this goal.
- **The spatial layout of components should be consistent from one frame to the next**. It is easier cognitively to maintain the correspondence between parts in one diagram frame and the next if a consistent view is used.
- **Actions should be illustrated along with connections between components**. Diagrams that showed the actions involved in assembly, rather than simply the three-dimensional layout of the parts, were much more effective. Arrows were used to show the placement of parts and dotted lines to show the addition of fasteners.

On the right is an example of a set of graphic instructions they produced according to their principles. People did better with these than with the manufacturer's instructions.

One might think that the narrative assembly diagram is a somewhat impoverished version of instructions that could be better presented using a videotape showing someone assembling the furniture correctly. This is not the case. The advantage of the narrative diagram is that it supports two different cognitive strategies. It supports the strategy of narrative, where the audience is taken through a series of cognitive steps in a particular order. It also supports a strategy, where the person using the diagram can construct and execute a mental model about which part is which and how they fit together for any step in the sequence. The user may look at

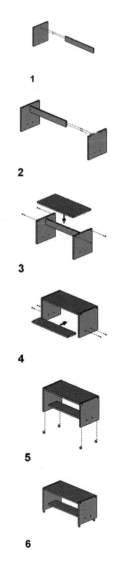

1

2

3

4

5

6

parts of the diagram at any time and in any order. A video presentation is less effective, because navigating through time in a video sequence is much more difficult than simply looking at different parts of a diagram sequence. Inevitably, the cognitive process gets out of sync with the video. The multiframe pictorial narrative is an important form because it better supports the construction and refinement of executable mental models.

COMBINING FIGURATIVE AND NON-FIGURATIVE ELEMENTS

In the panel below are three visualizations of the same data from Lydia Byrne and her coauthors.[•] Each shows the amount of harmful ultraviolet (UV) rays that may be received under different weather conditions. Contrary to expectations, when there are broken clouds there can be more dangerous UV illumination than when the sky is clear. The first

[•]L. Byrne, D. Angus, and J. Wiles, 2019. Figurative frames: A critical vocabulary for images in information visualization. *Information Visualization*. 18(1): 45–67.

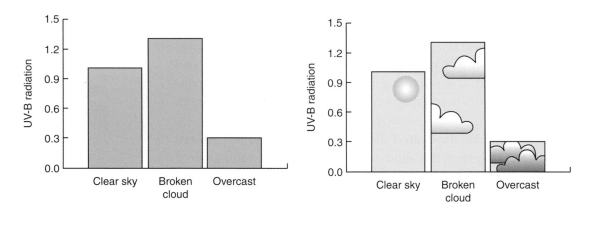

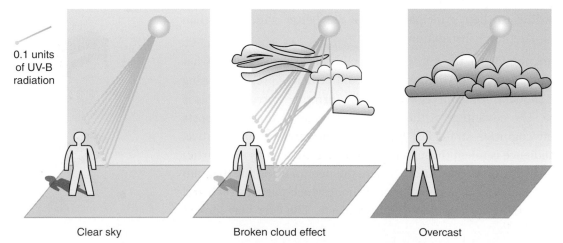

panel is a conventional bar chart representing the amounts of UV light under different conditions. In the second, the bars are labeled with figurative images, illustrating the conditions being represented. The third is the most interesting. It provides an explanation together with a representation of the quantitative values. This explanation relies on the construction of a mental model based on ray tracing.

In the case of scattered clouds, it can be seen that the human figure receives both direct rays from the sun and multipath rays scattered from the clouds. In the words of the creators of the figure, *"The lines have a figurative interpretation as rays from the sun which interact with clouds, but also have an abstract meaning as one-tenth of a unit of UV-B radiation received by the human recipient."* The graphic provides a basis for a predictive cognitive model which can be used in other situations. For example, when there is snow on the ground, many harmful rays may be reflected from the snow, almost doubling the exposure. Also, showing a human figure as the receiver of the rays makes it clear that it is people who should be concerned about having too much UV radiation. Animals, of course, can also be harmed by UV light, but this particular kind of graphic is probably more suitable for public education as a graphic explaining why people should use sunblock and wear big hats.

VISUALIZATIONS TO ADVERTISE

Sometimes the purpose of a visualization is not to convey a cognitive skill, but to impress its audience that the work is important. Simply put, it is advertising.

Pillar and Jets HH 901/902
Hubble Space Telescope • WFC3/UVIS

NASA, ESA, and M. Livio and the Hubble 20th Anniversary Team (STScI)   STScI-PRC10-13a

On the previous page is a heavily doctored image from the Hubble Space Telescope released by NASA. It is intended to promote the mental model in the minds of senators, congressmen, and the general public that this is important science and that NASA should continue to receive a large allocation of federal funding; scientists do not use these kinds of images to convey results to one another. Such images have obvious value as advertising, but it is important for the designer to be aware of what the goal is. It is often the case that visualization designers think they are being asked to help with the science of a project, whereas, in fact, they are being asked to simply show it off in a way that makes it look valuable and impressive. Both goals have value, but the kinds of designs that are appropriate are very different.

MAPS, PLANS, AND MENTAL MODELS WITH SPACE AND TIME

Maps can provide powerful tools in the construction of executable mental models. As discussed in Chapter 1, a subway map is a tool for planning future travel. Roadmaps are similar planning tools. Trip planning scenarios are often constructed and simulated through direct interaction with the map. Some web-based mapping tools support the simulation of trips made by car, public transportation, bicycle, or foot.

Weather maps delivered on the Internet have play-forward features supporting the modeling of future activities taking weather into account; sailors, hikers, and beachgoers rely on them. Longer-term weather maps based on climate change models support and augment longer-term predictive mental models.

Any presentation containing information about geographical space is likely to include a map. In most cases such maps will portray activities that occurred in the past, but the goal of the presentation should be to transmit skills regarding activities that audience members can undertake in the future. According to predictive mental model theory, saying "this is where we went to accomplish our goals," always contains an implicit message "this is how you, or someone else, might work in the future."

To give an example, at the top of the facing page is a globe showing the extent to which the ocean seabed has been mapped as of the beginning of the year 2020. It was created in support of the Seabed 2030 project, the goal of which is to fully map the oceans of the world by the year 2030.

On the globe, dark gray areas show what has not been mapped, whereas the brightly colored areas show what has been mapped. By early 2020 when the map was made, less than 20% of the oceans had been mapped.

The map highlights the need for an action plan which is easy to state, but difficult to execute: *"Go forth and map the oceans!"* Actually executing this plan involves ships, logistics, an extensive international organization, and billions of dollars. Like the Hubble image, part of its goal is advertising. But it also provides a tool which can be used to plan actual missions. Its use is simple: any dark gray area is in need of mapping.

NARRATIVE TENSION AND PLOT DEVELOPMENT

We usually think of plot construction as something practiced by writers of fiction, but nonfiction presentations also have a plot structure. In pulp fiction, one of the main goals is to maintain the audience in a state of anticipation that the story will end with momentous conflict resolving events. Presenters of dry technical subjects also have to convince an audience to pay attention.

When people follow a narrative, they build predictive mental models of possible worlds as they may unfold in the future. The need to keep in mind more than one alternative model is the source of dramatic tension.[•]

[•]A. Shirvani, S.G. Ware, and R. Farrell, 2017. A possible worlds model of belief for state-space narrative planning. *AAAI International Conference on Artificial Intelligence and Interactive Digital Entertainment.* 13(1), 101–107.

The brain is always trying to find simpler models to explain events and there is an implicit promise in most stories that a single explanation will eventually be provided; this is what holds the audience. Although the purpose of data presentation is to inform rather than entertain, the use of narrative tension can still be employed to advantage.

In science journalism a common plot device is the expedition. The audience is invited to follow a project whose goal is to find a solution to a scientific mystery. I was once part of a scientific cruise off the coast of Sumatra, the goal of which was to find the cause of the devastating tsunami that occurred in the year 2004. At the start of the resulting TV special, two candidate causes were proposed. It was already well established that a major fault had ruptured but there were two ways that this could have caused the giant waves. One alternative was a sudden uplift along one side of the fault line. The other was a massive submarine landslide triggered by the earthquake. Near the end of the show the issue was resolved—it was the uplift theory. The middle sections of the show were filled with clips of tension-building interviews with the scientists involved. There was a major side story concerning a deep submersible we sent down to investigate what was evidently the site of a major underwater landslide based on evidence from a sonar map we made. It turned out to be ancient, not recent, and therefore not the cause of the tsunami.

In written scientific papers, the results are typically announced at the very beginning in the form of an abstract, so there is little dramatic tension. If this were not done, savvy readers would skip to the conclusion section in any case. In the case of presentations given with slides, it is a good idea to introduce a measure of narrative tension at the start, although its heavy-handed use can be irritating. One common way of introducing basic plot tension is to propose alternative hypotheses, and visualizations can often be used to illustrate them. This may be done with simple cartoons or diagrams, or data displays showing the outcome of different theoretical predictions.

All presentations have a narrative structure, an introduction, a set of material in the middle where the ideas are elaborated, and a conclusion where the main findings and their implications are summarized.

The main goal of the introduction should be to bring a suite of mental models to a state of partial activation in the minds of the audience. This is done by setting up the context of the work. The subject of the presentation is first given in a broad way both with words and images. It is usually best to only hint at conclusions, so as to create some measure of dramatic tension. Sometimes prior work can be shown using visualizations and this can be a basis for explaining why there were unanswered and hopefully important questions. In particular, the use of potential causative agents encourages people to make predictions.•

The introductory part of a talk also should provide an answer to the question that audiences always have in mind, namely "Why should I care?" This can be done using images and words to create linkages to matters of general interest to a particular audience. These can range from broad societal issues to specific technical methods. All too often it is assumed that audience members will figure out the value for themselves and this can be a fatal error.

We tend to think of visualizations primarily for conveying information about data but, as we have seen in this chapter, there are many ways in which different kinds of visualizations can support mental model building. A simple cartoon can express the essence of a theory, and photographic images can convey the social or environmental context in which a theory applies; examples are factories, shops, urban settings, or groups of people engaged in particular activities. Through the powerful mechanism of "gist" (Chapter 6), visualizations rapidly activate the relevant model networks. If the work being discussed has a social or biological impact, images can be especially powerful. Diagrams can elucidate mechanisms, and, of course, conventional charts of various kinds can be used to show data.

Often in science, the narrative structure is a series of experiments, each with an introduction of theoretical principles, a description of experiments, and a description of results. In business, it may be series of case studies, or predictions based on business models followed with possible outcomes.

As with fiction, data narratives can contain more than one thread. In fictional narratives it is usual for two or three separate narratives to be interwoven. In nonfictional presentations, the use of interwoven narratives may also be worth doing if the conclusion can draw the threads together and thereby resolve the dramatic tension into a single, more unified model. However, we have limited cognitive resources to maintain multiple mental models. There are both costs and benefits to interweaving more than one thread. When complex ideas are being built step by step, switching context can have a substantial cost; if we are not careful, people may lose track of where they are in a particular story about data. To lessen the likelihood of this, switching the focus of attention from one model to another must always be clearly signaled, perhaps with reminders about where we are in this thread.

•N. Cohn and M. Paczynski, 2013. Prediction, events, and the advantage of Agents: The processing of semantic roles in visual narrative. *Cognitive Psychology. 67*(3): 73–97.

To sum up: conveying mental models is about expanding the realm of possible futures that can be imagined. Most people want to learn and understand a subject better, and the functional goal of any presentation should be to help them do so. The predictive cognition theory of presentation graphics focuses on what is important; namely, adding to the cognitive toolkits of the participating audience. If visualizations are to have an influence they must change people's behavior, and changing behavior starts with changing mental models.

Chapter 9

Creative Meta-seeing

When Michelangelo planned the frescoes for the Sistine Chapel ceiling he did not do it in his head or on the plaster. Instead the initial phases of creative work were done through the medium of thousands of sketches. These ranged from the highly speculative initial sketches to the finished paper designs that his assistants pricked through with black charcoal dust to transfer them to the still wet fresco plaster. Studies of how artists and designers work suggest that although the germ of an idea may often come in a reverie as a purely cognitive act, the major work of creative design is done through a kind of dialogue with some rapid production medium. Sketches have this function for the visual artist, rough clay or wax maquettes have the same function for the sculptor. Sketching is not confined to artists. Hastily drawn diagrams allow the engineer and scientist to "rough out" ideas; computer programmers sketch out the structure of computer programs. Many people, when they wish to organize their ideas, use pencil and paper to literally *draw* the links between labeled scribbles standing for abstract concepts.

Visual Thinking for Information Design. DOI: https://doi.org/10.1016/B978-0-12-823567-6.00009-4

This chapter is about the psychology of constructive visual thinking in the service of design. In addressing this subject we will encounter a number of fundamental questions. What is the difference between seeing and imagining? What is the difference between the visual thinking that occurs when we are making a sandwich, the visual thinking involved when we are reading a map, and the visual thinking we do when we are *designing* an advertising poster, a painting, or a website?

Although creative visual thinking can be almost infinitely varied, studies of designers, artists, and scientists have identified some common elements no matter what the tasks. We begin with a generalized view of the steps involved in the stages of the creative process.

Step 1—The visual concept is formed: Depending on the application, a graphic idea may be very free and imaginative or very stereotyped. An art director doing design for an advertising firm may be open to almost any new visual concept, so long as it can be somehow linked to the product and yield a positive association. Conversely, an architect designing an apartment building on a fixed budget is likely to have his visual imagination constrained to a small set of conventional alternatives. In either case the initial concept may be quite abstract and not particularly graphical. A "three-story, L-shaped building with twelve units" might be sufficient in the case of the architects.

Step 2—Externalization: A loose scribble is drawn on paper to externalize the concept and provide a starting point for design refinement.

Steps 2, 3, and 4 may be repeated many times.

Step 3—The constructive critique: The scribble is visual critiqued; some elements are visually tested. The designer performs a kind of informal cognitive task analysis, executing a series of visual queries to determine if the design meets requirements. As part of the process, new meanings may be bound with the external imagery and potential additions imagined.

Step 4—Consolidation and extension: The original scribble is modified. Faint existing lines may be modified or strengthened, consolidating the aspect of the design they represent. New lines may be added. Other lines may be erased, or may simply recede as other visual elements become stronger.

MENTAL IMAGERY

From the 1980s, two main theories of mental imagery have dominated. One, theory, championed by Zenon Pylyshyn, holds that mental imagery is purely symbolic and nonspatial.[•] Spatial ideas are held as *logical propositions* such as "the cup is on the table" or "the picture is to the left of the door." According to this view, there is *no spatial representation* in the brain in the sense of patterns of neural activation having some spatial correspondence to the arrangement of the objects in space.

[•]Z. Pylyshyn, 1973. What the mind's eye tells the mind's brain: A critique of mental imagery. *Psychological Bulletin*. 80: 1–25.

The second view, championed by Stephen Kosslyn, holds that mental imagery is constructed using the same neurological apparatus responsible for normal seeing.[•] These phantom images are constructed in the spatial neural maps that represent the visual field in various areas of the visual

[•]S. Kosslyn and J.R. Pomeranz, 1977. Imagery, propositions, and the form of internal representations. *Cognitive Psychology*. 9: 52–76

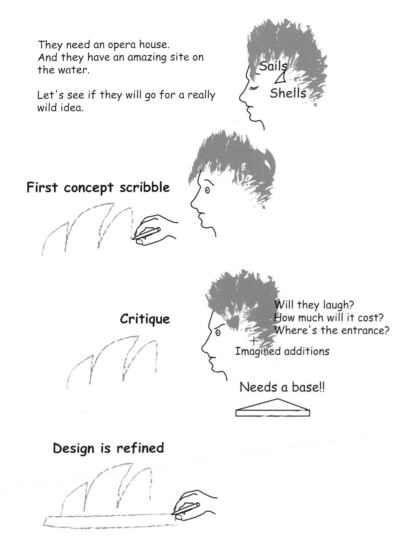

They need an opera house.
And they have an amazing site on
the water.

Let's see if they will go for a really
wild idea.

Sails

Shells

First concept scribble

Critique

Will they laugh?
How much will it cost?
Where's the entrance?

Imagined additions

Needs a base!!

Design is refined

cortex, forming an internal sketch that is processed by higher levels, much as external imagery is processed.

More recently a third view has emerged based on the idea that mental images are mental activities. This view has been set out clearly by a philosopher, N.J.T. Thomas of California State University. This is part of the revolution in thinking about perception that is sweeping cognitive science, and which inspired the creation of this book. According to this account, visual imagery is based on the same cognitive activities as normal seeing, hence it is sometimes called activity theory.[*]

Normal seeing is a constructive, task-oriented process whereby the brain searches the environment and extracts information as needed for the task at hand. Of course, mental images are not based on any

[*]N.J.T Thomas, 1999. Are theories of imagery theories of imagination? An active perception approach to conscious mental content. *Cognitive Science*, 23, 207–245.

immediate external information—that is their very definition—but they are based on the same constructive mental processes. They consist of the activities without the external information.

Understanding mental images is critical because design is a creative process wherein some activities are done as mental images, and some are done by a sort of hybrid between mental imagery and normal seeing where design elements are imagined and mentally added to incomplete sketches.

The whole process can be also thought of in terms of the predictive mental models which form the basis of the previous chapter. Only in some respects it goes beyond it in the sense that the mental models are distributed; partly they exist within the brain and partly they exist in the outside worlds.

Supporting the activity theory of mental imagery is the finding that eye movements occur when people "look at" mental images that are entirely in their heads. Moreover, the pattern of locations (although not the sequence) that the eyes fixate when viewing a scene is closely matched when a scene that has been previously viewed is mentally imaged.[*]

[*]B. Laeng and D.S. Teodorescu, 2002. Eye scanpaths during visual imagery reenact those of perception of the same visual scene. *Cognitive Science.* 26: 207–231.

Other support for activity theory comes from using functional magnetic resonance imaging (fMRI) to reveal which areas of the brain are active during mental imaging. fMRI studies show that much of the same brain

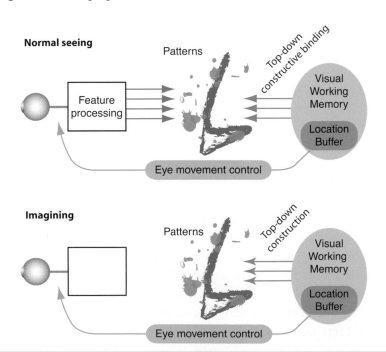

According to activity theory, the process of visual imagination uses the same high-level mechanisms as normal vision. Eye movements, although seemingly unnecessary, occur as part of the activity of imagining.

machinery is active when people imagine something visual as is active during normal seeing with the eyes open, at least in the higher visual processing areas.• On the other hand, fMRI also shows that the lower, primary visual cortex is *not* active during mental imagery. Since these lower areas are the obvious place for Kosslyn's phantom image to be created, this has been taken as evidence against the spatial sketchpad theory.

As discussed in Chapter 6, certain kinds of visual objects have their specialized brain areas. A brain area called the fusiform gyrus is essential for human face perception. fMRI studies show this area is active both when people see faces and when they mentally image them. Likewise, a region of the midbrain called the parahippocampal area is associated with perception of spatial locations. This area is also active in the creation of mental imagery.

•G. Ganis, W.L. Thompson, and S.M. Kosslyn, 2004. Brain areas underlying visual mental imagery and visual perception: an fMRI study. *Cognitive Brain Research*. 20: 226–241.

Perception   Imagery   Perception - Imagery

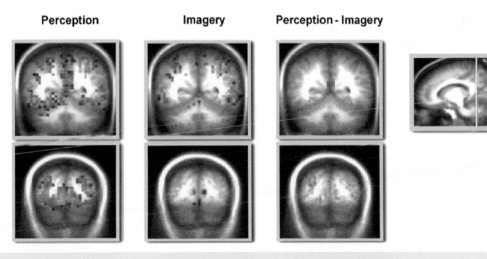

This fMRI image shows that in the higher levels of visual processing, for example in the parietal lobe area associated with active looking, very similar patterns of brain activation occur whether the person is actually looking at an image or imagining that same image. In the earlier stages of visual processing, at the back of the brain (second row), there is comparatively less activation of visual cortical areas when an image is imagined as opposed to seen.

Taken together the fMRI studies show that the same higher-level neural machinery is active during mental imaging as is active during seeing. But the lower-level machinery of the primary visual cortex (discussed in Chapter 2), is not active in mental imagery and this is why Kosslyn's account would seem to be at least partially wrong. According to Kosslyn's view, visual imagery is held at lower levels of the visual system and examined by higher levels, and the primary visual cortex is exactly the area where one would expect such a mental sketch to be held. Visual imagery seems to occur entirely in the higher levels of visual processing, using, among other things, the active spatial processes normally involved in the planning and execution of eye movements.

Mental imagery can therefore be thought of as an internalized active process; much as our inner dialogue is internalized speech, visual imagery is based on the internalized activities of seeing. Just as internalized speech can be used to plan future actions and interpret past ones in an active process, so internalized seeing can be used to plan and interpret as part of the design process.

However, there is a key difference—everyone uses internalized speech as a thinking tool, but the constructive internalization of mental imagery is a skill that is more specialized. Experienced designers will internalize the dialogue with paper, others who do not use sketching as a design tool will not.

Mostly, though, the process of design combines some of the cognitive activities of normal seeing with the activities of visual imagination. The particular unique process of design is a kind of *constructive* perception. This leads us to a critical cognitive tool of the designer, the line sketch.

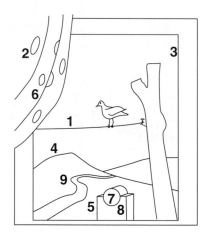

Lines representing:

1) A thin wire
2) A surface color boundary
3) An aperture
4) A silhouette contour for a
   rounded surface
5) A silhouette of a sharp edge
6) An internal contour
7) A crack between two
   abutting objects
8) An edge where two planes
   meet
9) A material boundary

THE MAGIC OF THE SCRIBBLE

Lines are capable of representing many different things as the above figure illustrates.[*] How can this chameleon quality be explained? The answer lies in the critical importance of edges in visual processing. As discussed in Chapter 3, a major function of early- and middle-stage visual processing is the extraction of continuous contours. An object may be separated from its background in many different ways including luminance changes at its silhouette, color differences, texture boundaries, and even motion boundaries. A generalized contour extraction mechanism in the pattern-processing stage of perception allows us to discern an object from many

[*]An extensive discussion of the expressive power of lines can be found in John M. Kennedy's book *The Psychology of Picture Perception*, Jossey Bass, 1974. Kennedy was my PhD thesis advisor.

kinds of visual discontinuity. Lines on paper provide a strong signal to this generalized contour mechanism with the consequence that something as abstract as a circle on paper can have five different meanings.

Five different objects with the same visual representation.

In this cartoon, Saul Steinberg exploits the chameleon quality of lines to represent many kinds and properties of objects. He also uses line quality as a way to express the whimsical chain of a child's monologue and the harsh abstract logic of the adult. (S. Steinberg, 1959, *Untitled*. Ink on paper. First published in the *New Yorker*, March 14, 1959. © The Saul Steinberg Foundation/ Artists Rights Society (ARS), New York.)

The Italian psychologist Manfredo Masseroni devised the following exercise for the reader to understand directly how the magic of lines can be used as part of a creative design process.• Make a simple scribble by moving a pen around in a large irregular looping pattern. Do not think about representing anything while you do it. You should end up with a few scribbles like the ones on the next page. To transform your meaningless scribbles into birds, just add a small circle ○ and a < shape to some loop of the scribble. Magically, a bird will appear and different parts of the scribble will suddenly become head, wings, tail, and body. What is remarkable about this exercise is that almost any scribble can become a bird.

Massironi, M. The Psychology of Graphic Images: Seeing, Drawing, Communicating. Psychology Press, Hove, UK, 2001.

The point of this exercise is twofold. First, it emphasizes the constructive power of seeing. Simple looping lines become wings and bodies. Second, and more importantly, it illustrates an important creative design technique that many artists and designers use and that, as we shall see, points at the essence of the way sketches function as creative tools.

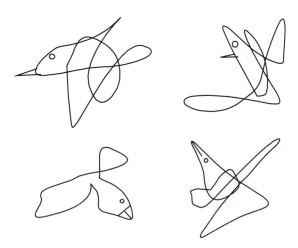

Alternatively, by adding slightly different features you should be able to create people or other animals.

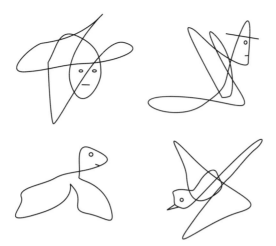

This mode of drawing can be used as a kind of visual brainstorming. You will undoubtedly come up with designs that are different from anything you would have deliberately produced had you proceeded more methodologically. And you may well find out that the results are livelier and visually more interesting. The deliberately "random'" scribble is often used by artists and designers as a way of liberating their creative process from stereotyped visual thinking. The perceptual mechanisms are exquisitely tuned to find meaning often from slender evidence, and this is why meaning is so readily found in meaningless scribbles.

DIAGRAMS ARE IDEAS MADE CONCRETE

A diagram differs from a sketch in that its purpose is to express concepts that need not be spatial in nature. Usually some of the concepts are denoted by words as well as graphical forms. Lines and other spatial elements are used as abstractions to connect more basic concepts into concept structures.

Diagrams are used to plan, design things, and structure ideas. Architects, computer software designers, engineers, and scientists use them as essential cognitive tools. Artist's notebooks are often full of diagrams that differ fundamentally from their sketches in that they are not visual *prototypes* for a finished piece of art; rather they are *expressions of concept structures*. The entities of a diagrammatic design will, in most cases, have very little resemblance to the things they represent. Diagrams often contain formalized components that have precise meanings. Examples are transistors and resistors in circuit diagrams, doors and windows in architectural drawings. Any specialized field typically has its own set of conventions. It is impossible to discuss the universe of such diagramming symbols because there are thousands of them in existence; often a single technical field will have several hundred specialized symbols. There is one kind of symbol, however, that merits special

This page, from the notebook of Charles Darwin, shows the first known illustration of the evolutionary tree concept. The visual structure, together with labels A, B, C, and D, is used to support reasoning about the evolutionary distance between different creatures.

The original notebook is in Cambridge University Library.

comment, because it is an abstraction used in many ways in many different kinds of diagrams. This is the arrow.

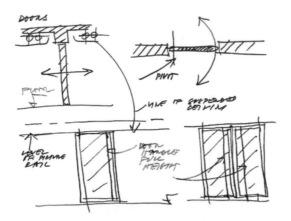

In this design diagram for doors, architect Eva Jiricna uses arrows in multiple ways including the motion path of a door, labeling of parts connecting verbally expressed ideas to parts of the graphic, and connecting different parts of the compound diagram. (Sketches by Eva Jiricna.)

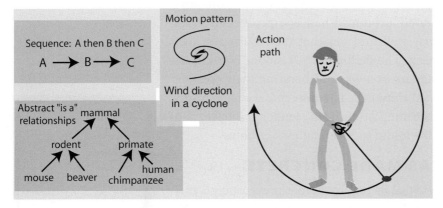

A few of the abstractions expressible through arrows

Arrows are interesting because of the way they allow the application of the powerful pattern-finding mechanisms of the visual system to be combined with a measure of abstract meaning. They can express motion paths, both historical and planned, as well abstract conceptual relationships of various types, including causal relationships, sequences, and taxonomic hierarchies. They can also simply direct attention to a particular feature of a diagram or photograph. The arrowhead has the purely symbolic function of showing directionality either in an abstract sense (the phrase "a mouse *is a* rodent" has a directionality in the sense that the converse is not true) or in the concrete sense of a direction of motion. In showing motion shaft of the arrow which can be either curved or shows a motion path, the arrow head is purely symbolic and shows which way along the path the motion is headed. In either case, this hybrid of a line pattern with a directional arrowhead can be rapidly scribbled, supporting the tight cognitive loop that is the essence of visual thinking through diagramming.

REQUIREMENTS AND EARLY DESIGN

Having considered the details of how lines function in visual thinking, it is necessary to return to the larger design process wherein the workload is distributed between the brain and visual tools.

The first part of any design process is an understanding of the requirements of the design. In some disciplines, such as engineering, this stage is explicit and well defined. In less constrained disciplines, a designer must still establish requirements and goals before examining potential solutions, although the process may be quite informal. The aim is to understand and define a problem before attempting to solve it. This can avoid the pitfall of becoming married to visually seductive, but inappropriate or ineffective solutions.

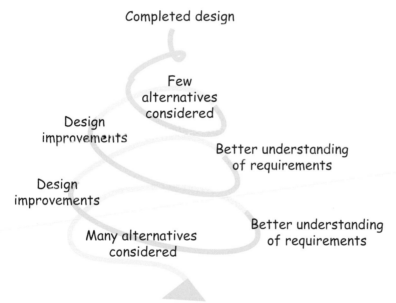

Often clients do not appreciate what is possible until they see an example.

Prototype designs can serve as a discussion point bringing in the opinions of many stakeholders in the project. At the next meeting the design is refined and presented again for further refinements.

Sometimes, however, the articulation of requirements goes hand in hand with the presentation of early design solutions. The process is called a *spiral design* methodology. Many clients can only appreciate design constraints when they are presented with partially realized alternatives, so having examples prepared is necessary to effective dialogue.

When spiral design is used, the requirements are only vaguely specified at first. Both the requirements and the design become more refined as the project proceeds. This has the advantage of enabling insights during later stages of the project to be incorporated. The major disadvantages are that it can be difficult to incorporate changes into a contract and deadlines may need to be altered.

Much specification of requirements is not inherently visual, but for those that are, a *visual task analysis* is required. This is an understanding of the visual cognitive operations the design is intended to support.

VISUAL TASK ANALYSIS

A visual task analysis consists of the identification of cognitive tasks that must be supported by a design. Once a set of tasks has been identified, they can be broken down further into a set of visual queries that will be executed by an individual in performing a cognitive task with the product. For example, a firm of landscape architects might produce design sketches to reason about how the garden will function for the people who will ultimately use it. Tasks include reasoning about affordances for walking along paths and over lawns, and the need for patio space and flower beds. Visual queries relating to walking or strolling will be best supported by a design allowing for paths, lawns, and patios to be perceivable as visual gestalt through the careful use of color, texture, or line.

THE CREATIVE DESIGN LOOP

In a landmark study of the creative design process, Masaki Suwa from the Hitachi Research Laboratory in Japan and Barabara Tversky of Stanford University asked a set of advanced architecture students to design an art museum. The students were videotaped while they sketched designs and later asked to watch their own tapes and comment on what they had been thinking. This study revealed that the designers would often start with a very loose sketch, usually of a ground-level layout, then *interpret what they had set down.* They did not just formulate ideas in their heads and then set these ideas on paper. The process of sketching was itself a constructive act. The sketch had the function of dividing the paper into regions of *potential* architectural meaning. A line might be considered at one moment as the boundary of a room, or it might come cognitively to represent the edge of a sculpture garden at one side of a building. Suwa and Tversky later called this *constructive perception* and suggested that it is fundamental to the design process.•

Experienced architects are also prolific sketchers. Bryan Lawson conducted a series of interviews with six leading architects to gain an understanding of how they worked.• Of the Spanish architect, Santiago Calatrava, he wrote: "Calatrava is an accomplished artist with a fine sense of line and texture, but one senses that his graphical output is never the result of a wish to produce a drawing *but rather to understand a problem*" [emphasis mine].

•M. Suwa and B. Tversky, 2003. Constructive perception: A metacognitive skill for coordinating perception and conception. *Cognitive Science Society Proceedings.* 25, 1140–1144.

•B. Lawson. 1994. *Design in Mind.* Architectural Press. Oxford.

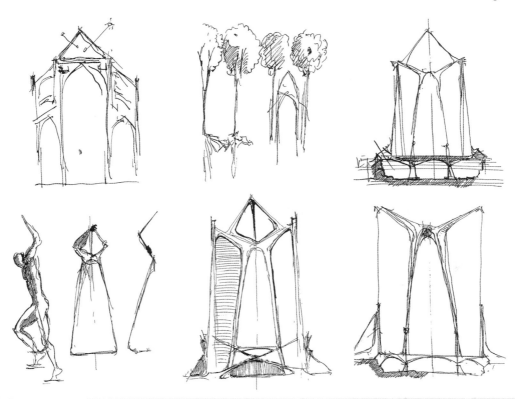

A few sample sketches from Calatrava's notebooks show trees, the human form, and traditional architectural forms, all being used as sources of inspiration for the design of the roof truss system of a modern cathedral. Each of the examples explores a different idea. In some a metaphorical comparison of forms (the male figure and the tree) is the primary focus. Others are explorations of abstract forms that can meet the structural requirements of a building. (Sketches by Santiago Calatrava.)

One of the most critical characteristics of a sketch is the speed with which it can be produced, and this means that it can also be discarded with little cost. A designer may easily produce twenty or thirty sketches to find the solutions to various problems, and retain only one.

A vague concept

A loose scribble on paper

Add marks
to extend or consolidate
design

Visually scan and constructively
interpret the scribble
Mentally project additions to
the scribble

COGNITIVE ECONOMICS OF DESIGN SKETCHING

Which cognitive operations are carried out purely in the head through mental imagery, and which cognitive operations result in marks on paper, can be understood partially in terms of cognitive economics. We can shuffle visual concepts in and out of visual working memory several times a second. Adding a mark to a sketch takes longer, a second or two to preserve an idea that would otherwise be lost. Visual working memory is the most flexible, high-speed sketchpad, but has very limited capacity and is very impermanent. Rough sketches on paper have less flexibility, but they also support greater complexity and can be kept or rapidly discarded. Permanent detailed designs have the least flexibility, cost a lot to produce, but can be very elaborate. As the design process progresses, the kinds of design artifacts that are produced may change from many low-cost sketches to a few high-cost, detailed, and finished drawings.

It is known from human memory research that recognition is vastly easier than recall. In other words, we can recognize that we have seen something before far more easily than we can reconstruct a memory. It is similarly true that identifying an effective design is vastly easier than creation of that same design. In a sense this is not surprising, it takes but a few seconds to appreciate, at least superficially, that one is in the presence of an interesting and visually exciting design. But this suggests that it is useful to have a design production method that can produce lots of designs at least semi-automatically. Then our job is to select from them, equally rapidly.

THE PERCEPTUAL CRITIQUE

As the designer quickly creates a conceptual design sketch, an ongoing perceptual critique is occurring. This can be thought of as a form of meta-seeing in that it is critical and analytic in a way that goes beyond the normal process of visual thinking associated with everyday tasks. It involves the interpretation and visual analysis of the marks on the paper that have just been put down.

There are two kinds of preliminary design artifacts that we have been considering and each involve different forms of meta-seeing. The first, the *concept diagram*, is about design concepts and usually has little in common with the appearance of any physical object. An example of this would be Darwin's sketch of the evolutionary tree. The second is the *prototype design* which is a rough version of a final product. An example of this would be a rough sketch of a poster or a web page. Many of the most interesting diagrams are combinations of the two. For example, a landscape architect will create sketches that have a rough spatial correspondence to where flower beds and lawns will appear in a finished garden. Many parts of the sketch and the cognitive operations it supports will be highly abstract and conceptual. For example, arrows showing strolling routes.

Designs are tested by means of functional visual queries. For example, a visual query can establish the distance between design elements and thereby discover if an element representing an herb garden is an appropriate distance from an element representing the house. Similar visual queries might be made regarding the area of the lawn, the location of pathways, and the shapes and distributions of flowerbeds. In each case, the corresponding elements are brought into visual working memory, and tested in some way, by means of judgment of distance, area, or shape.

The graphical marks that represent a rose garden in one instant may be reconsidered in the next as representing a space for an herb garden. The cognitive operation is a change in the bindings between visual working memory objects and verbal working memory objects.

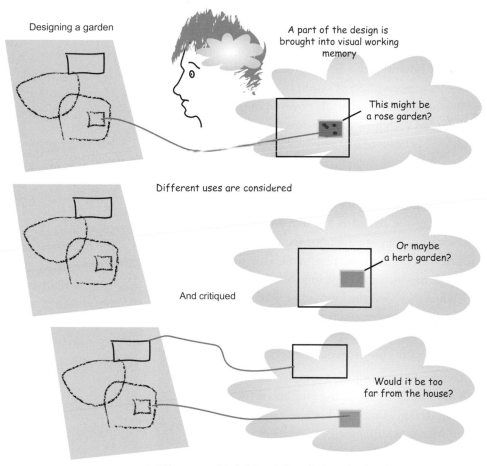

Designing a garden

A part of the design is brought into visual working memory

This might be a rose garden?

Different uses are considered

Or maybe a herb garden?

And critiqued

Would it be too far from the house?

A different graphical object is brought into visual working memory as attention shifts to the relationship between the "herb garden" rectangle and the rectangle representing the house.

Purely cognitive visual imagery can be added to the visual working memory representation of parts of the design. A paved path might be imagined as part of the design. In this case part of what is held in visual working memory corresponds to marks on the paper, whereas the additions are pure mental images. The very limited capacity of visual working memory requires that imagined additions are simple. In order to extend the design in an elaborate way, the imagined additions must be added to the scribble. However, because mental additions have a far lower cognitive cost than adding to the drawing, many additions can be imagined for every graphical addition to the sketch. Mental deletions can similarly be proposed, and occasionally consolidated by erasing or scribbling over some part of the sketch.

META-SEEING WITH DESIGN PROTOTYPES

The design prototype is a rapid sketch that shows in some respects what a finished product will actually look like. In the case of a proposed layout for a web page it might suggest a possible set of colors and the locations of various information boxes. The perceptual critique of a design prototype can be used for direct tests of how well the design will support cognitive tasks. These have to do with the perception of symbols, regions, and contours, and the details of this have been extensively covered in the previous chapters. Now we are concerned with how the low-level pattern finding is integrated into the higher-level process of meta-seeing.

The designer who is doing a quick conceptual sketch has a problem. Critiquing something that you yourself have produced is much more difficult than critiquing something someone else has produced. You, the designer, already know where each part of the design is located—you put those elements in place and you know what they are intended to signify. Perceiving it from the point of view of a new viewer is a specialized skill. This, in essence, is a kind of cognitive walkthrough in which you must simulate in your own mind what other people will see when they view the finished product. This involves simulating the visual queries that another person might wish to execute and asking of yourself questions such as, "Is this information sufficiently distinct," and "Does the organization support the proper grouping of concepts?"

To some extent self-critiquing can improve simply through the passage of time. After 2 or 3 days the priming of the circuits of the brain that occurred during the original design effort will have mostly dissipated and fresh alternatives can be more readily imagined.

Sometimes a more formal analysis of a design may be warranted. This requires a detailed breakdown of cognitive tasks, to be performed with a design. Each task is then used as the basis for a *cognitive walkthrough* of the prototype design using people who are not designers but potential consumers of the design. The process involves considering each task individually, determining the visual queries that result, then thinking through the execution of those queries. For example, if the design is a road map, then the queries might involve assessing whether the major roads connecting various cities can easily be traced.

Doing cognitive walkthroughs with other participants has a very high cost of time and effort. The combined amount of cognitive work is high and typically only justified for more finished designs. Many early design sketches may not be good solutions and must be rejected. The principle of cognitive economy dictates that designers must develop visual skills that help them to assess designs at an early stage without involving other participants.[*]

VISUAL SKILL DEVELOPMENT

Many designers are not aware of their critical analytic thought processes, any more than we are aware of the skills we have when buttering a piece of bread. It is so long since we first learned to do it that we have completely forgotten that stage at which the task required intense concentration. This is why the expert is often intolerant of the novice. He simply does not understand how an apparently obvious design flaw can be overlooked. But the ability to do a visual critique is an acquired skill.

All skilled behavior proceeds from the effortful to the automatic. For example, at the early stages of learning to type it is necessary to conduct a visual search for every key, and this consumes so much visual, procedural, and motor capacity that nothing is left over for composing a paragraph. At the expert level the finger movement sequences for whole words have become automatic and composing on the keyboard seems completely natural. Very little high-level cognitive involvement is needed and so visual and verbal working memory are free to deal with the task of composing the content of what is to be written.

The progression from high-level effortful cognition to low-level automatic processing has been directly observed in the brain by Russel Poldrack and a team at the University of California who used fMRI to study the development of a visual skill.[*] For a task, they had subjects read mirror-reversed text, which is an early-stage skill for most people. They found that parts of the brain involved in the task were from the temporal lobe areas of the brain associated with conscious effortful visual attention. In contrast, reading normal text, which is a highly automated learned skill, only caused brain activity in lower-level pattern recognition areas of the cortex.

It takes time to convert the hesitant effortful execution of tasks into something that is done automatically in the brain but it is not simply practice time that counts. A number of studies show that sleep is critical to the process. Skills only become more automatic if there is a period of sleep between the episodes where the skill is practiced. This has shown to be the case for many different tasks: for texture discriminations that might be

[*]For a full of account of the cognitive walkthrough methodology, see C. Wharton, J. Reiman, C. Lewis, and P. Polson, 1994. *The Cognitive Walkthrough Method: A Practitioner's Guide.* New York: Wiley.

[*]R. A. Poldrack, J.E. Desmond, G.H. Glover, and J.D.D. Gabrieli, 1998. The neural basis of visual skill learning: and fMRI study of mirror reading. *Cerebral Cortex.* 8(1): 1–10.

important in judging the quality of cloth, in typing letter sequences, and in tasks, like riding a bicycle, that require physical dexterity. Thus, we may practice a task for hours and gain little benefit; but if we practice for only half an hour, then wait a day, some measure of *automaticity* will be gained.

It is not enough that we simply go through the motions in learning visual analytic skills. Whatever is to be learned must be the focus of attention. A couch potato may watch television soap operas for hours every day over years but learn nothing about the skills of film directing. However, a director will see, and *interpret the value of*, lighting, camera angles, and shot sequences. The important skills for the designer are interpreting and constructive criticism. It is not enough to look at many visual designs; each must be subjected to a visual critique for these skills to develop. This book is intended to provide perceptually based design rules that form one basis for critical assessment.

CONCLUSION

The skill of thinking through sketching has nothing to do with the ability to draw in the conventional sense of drawing a portrait or a landscape. The vaguest scribble can augment the process of constructive visual thinking. The power of sketching in the service of design comes from the visual interpretive skills of the scribbler and their ability to use creative meta-seeing for the construction of both design ideas and mental models. Prototype design sketches allow for preliminary design ideas to be critiqued, both by the creator and by others. A concept sketch differs from a prototype sketch in that it is a method for constructing, organizing, and critiquing ideas. It provides abstract representations of ideas and idea structures. Most sketches are hybrids of prototype and concept sketches, partly appearance and partly ideas.

The power of sketching as a thinking tool comes from a combination of four things. The first is the fact that a line can represent many things because of the flexible interpretive pattern-finding capability of the visual system. The second has to do with the way sketches can be done quickly and just as easily discarded. Starting over is always an option. The third is the critical cognitive skill of interpreting lines in different ways. Part of this skill is the ability to project new ideas onto a partially completed scribble. Part of it is the ability to critique the various interpretations by subjecting them to functional visual queries. The fourth is the ability to mentally image new additions to a design and their meanings. Despite the fact that no significant drawing skill is needed, thinking with sketches is not easy. The skill to visually analyze either prototype designs or idea structures is hard won and it is what differentiates the expert from the novice designer. A whole lifetime's experience enriches a scribble and transforms it from a few meaningless marks to a thinking tool.

Chapter 10

The Dance of Meaning

Meaning is what the brain performs in a dance with the external environment. In this dance tokens of meaning are spun off into electronic and social media and tokens of meaning are likewise picked up. New meaning is constructed when patterns already stored within the brain are combined with patterns constructed from external information. Increasingly, new meaning is also constructed by inanimate computers that do at least partial analysis and synthesis of patterns and tokens of meaning, and then present the results using a visual display.

In this book, the dance partners are considered to be individual people interacting with visual displays. In reality the dance is far more intricate and ELABORATE; there is a constant stream of new meaning being developed by people interacting with one another. Visual thinking is but a small part of the dance. Nevertheless, because of the special power of the visual system as a pattern-finding engine, visual thinking has an increasingly important role. This book itself is part of the dance, as is everything that is designed to be accessed visually.

Visual Thinking for Information Design. DOI: https://doi.org/10.1016/B978-0-12-823567-6.00010-0

One of the main themes we have explored in this book is that at every level of description visual thinking can be thought of as active processes operating through the neural machinery of the brain, which, through interconnections and neuron firing patterns, embody executable models controlling our interactions with the world. The purpose of this chapter is to review and summarize what we have covered so far and then discuss some of the broader implications of how the theory of perception applies to design.

REVIEW

The following few pages give a twelve-point summary of the basic machinery and the major processes involved in visual thinking. With the twelfth point we shall segue into observations that go beyond what has been said before.

1. The eye has a small high-resolution area of photoreceptors called the fovea. We see far more detail in the fovea than off to the side and we sample the world by making rapid eye movements from point to point. Eye movements rotate the eyeball so that imagery from different parts of the visual world falls on the fovea to be analyzed by the brain.

2. Our brains construct visual queries to pick up what is important to support what we are doing cognitively at a given instant. Queries trigger rapid eye movements to enable us to pick up information that answers the query.

How affluent?

What are their ages?

"Unexpected Returns" by Ilya Repin, taken from A. Yarbus, 1967. Eye movements during perception of complex objects. L.A. Riggs, ed., *Eye Movements and Vision*, Plenum Press. NY. Chapter VII, 171–196.

On the previous page is a picture by the Russian realist painter Ilya Repin titled, "They did not expect him." Further to the right, shown in red, are eye movement traces from one person asked to perform different analytic tasks. When asked about the material well-being of the family, the eye movements fixate on clothes, pictures on the walls, and other furnishings (top). When asked about the ages of the family members, the eye movements fixate on faces almost exclusively (bottom).

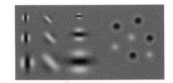

3. The first stage of cortical visual processing is a local feature analysis done simultaneously for every part of the visual field. The orientation, size, color, and motion of each part of the image falling on the retina are determined all at once by feature selective neurons. Smaller-scale features are only analyzed in the fovea at the center of vision. All other visual processing is based on the initial division of the visual world into features.

These records were made by the Russian psychologist Alfred Yarbus, who in 1967 used a mirror attached by means of a suction cup to his subjects' eyeballs to reflect light onto photographic paper and thereby record eye movements.

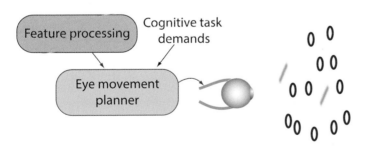

Understanding feature-level processing tells us what will stand out and be easy to find in a visual image. In the image above, the green bars are distinct in terms of several feature dimensions: color, orientation, curvature, and sharpness. We can easily execute eye movements to find the green bars because orientation, color, and curvature are all feature properties that are processed at an early stage, and early-stage properties are the ones that can be used by the brain in directing eye movements.

A simple motion pattern can also be thought of as a feature. Something that moves in a field of mostly static things is especially distinctive and easy to find.

4. There are two major processing pathways called the *where* and *what* pathways.

   The *where* pathway has connections to various regions in the parietal lobe responsible for visually guided actions, such as eye movements, walking, and reaching to grasp objects.

   The *what* pathway is responsible for identifying objects through a series of stages in which increasingly complex patterns are processed, each stage building on the previous one.

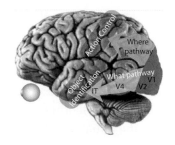

Between the *low-level* feature analysis and *high-level* object recognition is an intermediate pattern-finding stage. This divides visual space into regions bounded by a contour and containing similar textures, colors, or moving features. In V4 more complex compound shapes are identified from patterns of features. In the inferotemporal cortex, neurons respond to specific meaningful patterns such as faces, hands, letters of the alphabet, and automobiles.

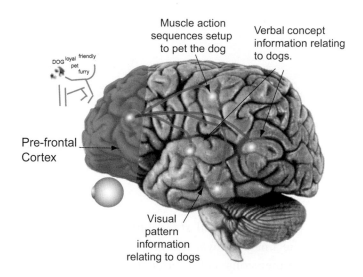

5. As we think visually, various kinds of information are combined in temporary nexuses of meaning. This information can include visual pattern information, language-based concepts, and action patterns. Nexuses are short lived and they make up the contents of the working memories.

From one to three meaningful nexuses can be formed every time we fixate on a part of a scene. Some of these may be held from one eye fixation to the next, depending on their relevance to the thought process. This three-object visual working memory limit is a basic bottleneck in visual thinking.

6. One way that visual displays support cognition is by providing aids to memory. Small images, symbols, and patterns can provide *proxies* for concepts. When these proxies are fixated, the corresponding concepts become activated in the brain. This kind of visually triggered activation can often be much faster than retrieval of the same concept from internal long-term memory without such aids. When an external concept proxy is available, access to it is made by means of eye movements which typically take approximately one-tenth of a second. Once the proxy is fixated, a corresponding concept is activated within less than two-tenths of a second. It is possible to place upwards of thirty concept proxies in the form of images, symbols, or patterns on a screen providing a very quickly accessible concept buffer. Compare this to the fact that we can hold only approximately three concept chunks in visual or verbal working memory at a time. There is a major limitation to this use of external proxies—it only works when there are learned associations between the visual symbols, images, or patterns and particular concepts.

House 2

imac1

Airport

Men

Parking

Phone

Special

Women

CSS

Bicycle

Fire

Help

Radiactive

Recycle

School

How did the information get from Mark to Briana?

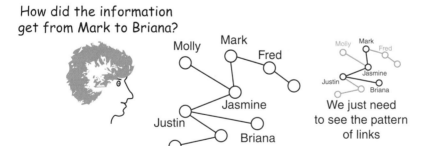

Molly Mark Fred Jasmine Justin Briana

We just need to see the pattern of links

7. Another way in which visual displays support cognition is through pattern finding. Visual queries lead to pattern searches and seeing a pattern, such as a connection between two objects, often providing the solution to a cognitive problem.

8. Language processing is done through specialized centers in the left temporal lobe. Language understanding and production systems are specialized for a kind of informal logic exemplified by the "ifs," "ands," and "buts" of everyday speech. This is very different and complementary to the visual logic of pattern and spatial arrangements.

9. The term "attention" is used to refer to the focus of brain activity as a particular moment. This focus is multifaceted and can be externally or internally controlled. At the early stage of visual processing, attention biases the patterns which will be constructed from raw imagery. Different aspects of the visual images are enhanced or suppressed according to the top-down demands of the cognitive thread. An art critic's visual cortex at one moment may be tuned to the fine texture of brush strokes, at another to the large-scale composition of a painting, and at yet another to the color contrasts. Attention is also the very essence of eye-movement control because looking is a prerequisite for attending. When we wish to attend to something, we point our eyeballs at it so that the next little bit of the world we are most interested in falls on the fovea. The planning of eye movements is therefore the planning of the focus of attention, and the sequence of eye fixations is intimately tied to the thread of visual thinking.

Visual working memory is a process that is pure attention. It is a momentary binding together of a few nexuses of visual features and patterns that seem most relevant to the cognitive thread. These constructions are short lived, most lasting only a tenth of a second, or less than the duration of a single fixation. A few persist through a series of successive fixations, being reconnected to the appropriate parts of the visual image after each one. Some visual working memory constructions are purely imaginary and not based on external imagery. When an artist is contemplating a stroke of a pen, or an engineer is contemplating the alteration of a design, mentally imaged potential marks on the paper can be combined with information from the existing sketch. The combination of imaginary with the real is what makes visual thinking such a marvel and is a key part of the internal-external dance of cognition.

There is a basic cycle of attention. Between one and three times a second our brains query the visual environment, activate an eye movement to pick up more information, process it, and re-query. The information picked up becomes the content of visual working memory. This cycle provides the basic low-level temporal structure of the cognitive thread. At a higher level the cognitive thread can have a wide variety of forms. Sometimes the cognitive thread is largely governed by external information coming through the senses. In the case of a movie, the cinematographer, directors, and actors can, to a large extent, control the cognitive thread of the audience. This is not to deny each person in an audience their own thoughts and opinions about what they are seeing, but they will mostly look at the same images, and even the same parts of those images, in the same order. The objects constructed in a hundred people's visual and verbal working memories will be similar and occur in the same order.

Most of the time our visual cognitive thread is occupied with mundane things, like finding the path in front of us, picking up an object, or watching someone's face as they talk so as to integrate information from their facial expression with what they are saying. These skills are highly learned and so most of the time we are not aware of doing them; nevertheless, they do take up our attentional capacity.

Sometimes the cognitive thread is up for grabs. Someone walking, bored, along a flat unobstructed sidewalk only requires a small amount of visual attention to keep to the path and the rest of his or her attentional capacity is a kind of free resource. Such a person is likely to give a second glance to anything that is even slightly novel, especially if it is moving.

There is also the visual thinking process that occurs when someone reasons with a graphic design as an external aid. A map reader is carrying out a very goal-directed query loop that involves both the rough logic of the language-processing system together with the pattern-finding capability of the visual system.

To add to the diversity of attention, the cognitive thread shifts back and forth between visual-processing and language-processing modalities. Sometimes it is primarily visual, or visual and motor, as when we are doing something like tracing out a line with a pen. Sometimes it is driven by the language modules of the brain. We cannot do more than one visual task at a time, and we cannot do more than one verbal task at a time. But we can carry out a verbal task, such as talking on a cell phone, and another visual motor task, like folding laundry, at the same time, if one of them is a highly learned skill. The separation is not perfect and people driving while talking on phones are undoubtedly more dangerous, but these are examples of real multitasking using visual and verbal channels to semi-independently carry out two cognitive tasks at once. Nevertheless, it is when visual and language modalities are combined that the brain is most effective. A well-designed presentation, for example, will use words and graphics, each to convey different kinds of information and the two kinds of information will be linked using pointing, or simple proximity in space and time.

The natural way of linking spoken words and images is through deixis (pointing). People point at objects just prior to, or during, related verbal statements, enabling the audience to connect the visual and verbal information into a visual working memory nexus.

10. One basic skill of designers can be thought of as a form of constructive seeing. Designers can mentally add simple patterns to a sketch to test possible design changes before making any changes to the sketch.

11. Long-term episodic memories are executable predictive mental models, rather than fixed repositories like books or CD ROMs. Their primary purpose is action, not reminiscing. The pathways that are activated when a cognitive task is carried out become stronger if that task is successfully completed. These pathways exist in all parts of the brain and on many levels; they are responsible for feature detection, pattern detection, eye movement control, and the sequencing of the cognitive thread. Activated long-term memories are partially reconstructions of prior sequences of neural activity in particular pathways. Certain external or internal information can trigger these sequences. In the case of pattern recognition, the sequences are triggered by visual information sweeping up the "what" pathway.

Some visual skills, such as seeing closed shapes bound by contours as "objects" or understanding the emotional expressions of fellow humans, are basic in the sense that they are to some extent innate and common to all humans, although such skills are refined with practice and experience.

Understanding this scene requires the ability to perceive social interactions. (Photo: Josh Eckels)

Most importantly, long-term memories enable us to plan and act through their execution. We cannot do anything without having some ideas of the consequences of our actions.

Visual thinking is based on a hierarchy of skills. Sophisticated cognitive skills build on simpler ones. We cannot begin to play chess until we can identify the pieces, and we will not become an expert until we have learned patterns involving whole configurations relating to strategic advantage or danger. As we get skilled at a particular task, like chopping onions, the operation eventually becomes semiautomatic. This frees up our higher-level control processes to deal with higher-level problems, such as how to deal with an extra person coming to dinner. The process whereby cognitive activities become automated is absolutely critical in the development of expertise because of the fundamental limitations of visual and verbal working memory capacities. If a set of muscle movements involved in drawing a circle on paper becomes automated, then the designer has free capacity to deal with arrangements of circles.

Patterns of neural activation are not static configurations, but sequences of firing. At the highest levels, involving the prefrontal cortex at the front of the brain and the hippocampus in the middle, these sequences can represent action plans. This, too, is hierarchical. Complex tasks, like cooking a meal, involve high-level plans that have the end goal of getting food on the table, together with mid-level plans, like peeling and mashing potatoes, as well as with low-level plans that are semiautomatic, such as reaching for and grasping a potato.

Other perceptual tasks, such as reading a contour map, understanding a cubist painting, and interpreting an X-ray image, require specialized pattern recognition skills. These higher-level skills are much easier to acquire if they build on more basic skills, which means that an artist cannot be too radical and still expect to be widely understood.

12. Effective presentations based on visualization consist of the transmission of predictive mental models from the presenter to the audience. To be successful they must build on existing mental models.

There are many kinds of visualization that can help with this, from simply presenting data, to using cartoons and animation showing how things work, to photographs that provide rich information about the complexity of some part of the world.

———————————————

The sum of the cognitive processing that occurs in problem solving is moving inexorably from being mostly in the head, as it was millennia ago before writing and paper, to being a collaborative process that occurs partly in the heads of individuals and partly in computer-based cognitive tools. Computer-based cognitive tools are developing with great speed in human society, far faster than the human brain can evolve. Any routine cognitive task that can be precisely described can be programmed and executed on a computer, or on millions of computers. This is like the automation of a skill that occurs in the brain of an individual, except that the computer is much faster and less flexible.

A cognitive tool can be a map or a movie poster, but increasingly cognitive tools are interactive and computer based. This means that every visual object shown on the screen can be informative in its own right, as well as be a link, through a touch or mouse click, to more information. We may also be able to manipulate that information object with our computer mouse, to literally organize our ideas.

IMPLICATIONS

The active vision model has four broad implications for design.

1. Designs should support the pattern-finding capability of the brain. Information structures should be transformed into easily identified patterns.
2. Designs optimize the cognitive process as a nested set of activities.
3. Designs should take the economics of cognition into account, considering the cost of learning new tools and ways of seeing.
4. Designs should take the mental models of the consumers into account.

The following sections elaborate these principles with examples.

DESIGN TO SUPPORT PATTERN FINDING

Properly exploiting the brain's ability to rapidly and flexibly discover visual patterns can provide a huge payoff in design. The following example, from my own work, illustrates this. Over the past few years I have been fortunate to be involved in a project to discover the underwater behavior of humpback whales. The data was captured by a tag attached to a whale with suction cups. When the tag came off it floated to the surface and was retrieved. Each tag provided several hours of data on the position and orientation of the whale as it foraged for food at various depths in the ocean. This gave us an unprecedented opportunity to see how humpback whales behave when they are out of sight underwater.

Our first attempt to provide an analysis tool was to create a program that allowed ethologists to *replay* a moving three-dimensional model of the whale at any desired rate.* They were initially thrilled because for the first time they could see the whale's underwater behavior. Some fascinating and previously unknown behavioral patterns were identified by looking at these replays. Nevertheless, although the visualization tool did its job, analysis was extremely time-consuming. It took many hours of watching to interpret an hour's worth of data.

*This work is described in C. Ware, R. Arsenault, M. Plumlee, and D. Wiley, 2006. Visualizing the underwater behavior of humpback whales. *IEEE Computer Graphics & Applications.* July/August issue. 14–18.

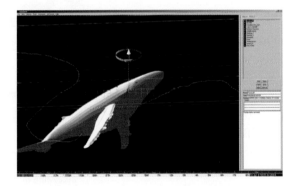

GeoZu4D software allows for the underwater behavior of a humpback whale to be played back along with any sounds recorded from a tag attached to the whale by means of suction cups.

Using this replay tool, the visual thinking process can be roughly summarized as follows. The whale movements were replayed by an ethologist looking for *stereotyped temporal sequences of movements*. When something promising was observed, the analyst had to remember it in order to identify similar behaviors occurring elsewhere in a record. The ethologist continued to review the replay looking for novel characteristic movement patterns.

Although this method worked, identifying a pattern might take three or four times as long as it took to gather the data in the first place. An 8-hour record from the tag could take days of observation to interpret. If we consider the problem in cognitive terms the reason becomes clear. We can remember at most only a half dozen temporal patterns in an hour of video, and these may not be the important or stereotyped ones. Further, we are not nearly as good at identifying and remembering motion patterns as we are at remembering spatial patterns. Also, every time an ethologist formed the hypothesis that some behavior might be stereotypical, it was necessary to review the tracks of all the other whales again looking for instances of the behavior that might have been missed.

Our second attempt at an analysis tool was far more successful because it took much greater advantage of the brain's pattern-finding ability. We transformed the track of the whale into a 3D ribbon. We added a sawtooth pattern above and below the ribbon that was derived from calculated accelerations indicating the fluke strokes of a whale.

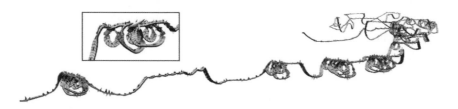

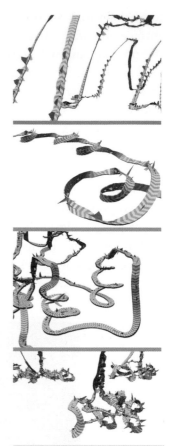

Ribbons make the underwater behavior of a humpback whale accessible through pattern perception.

Transforming the whale track into a ribbon allowed for much more rapid identification of behavior patterns. This new tool enabled a much different visual thinking process. The ethologist could quickly zoom in on a region where feeding behaviors were seen and stop to view a static image. Behavior patterns could be identified by visually scanning the image looking for repeated graphic patterns. Because eye movements are so fast and static patterns can be picked out efficiently, this method enabled analysts to compare several patterns *per second*. This process was hundreds of times faster than the replay method. Naturally, a complete analysis still took a great deal of work, but now we could scan the data for familiar or new patterns within minutes of extracting the data files from the tag. The new visual thinking process was hundreds of times faster than the old one based on simple replay.

The whale behavior study clearly demonstrates the general principle that patterns can be identified and compared very rapidly if we can turn information into the right kind of spatial display. The design challenge is to transform data into a form where the important patterns are easy to interpret.

OPTIMIZING THE COGNITIVE PROCESS

Good design optimizes the visual thinking process. The choice of patterns and symbols is important so that visual queries can be efficiently processed by the intended viewer. This means choosing words and patterns each to their best advantage. When designing the visual interface to an interactive computer program we must also decide how the visual information should change in response to every mouse click.

Extraordinarily powerful thinking tools can be made when a visual interface is added to a computer program. These are often highly specialized—for example, for stock market trading or engineering design. Their power comes from the fact that computer programs are cognitive processes that have been standardized and translated into machine-executable form. They offload cognitive tasks to machines, just as mechanical devices, like road construction equipment, offload muscle work to machines. Once offloaded, standardized cognitive tasks can be done blindingly fast and with little or no attention. Computer programs do not usually directly substitute for visual thinking, although they are getting better at that too; instead they take over tasks carried out by humans using the language-processing parts of the brain, such as sophisticated numerical calculations. A visual interface is sometimes the most effective way for a user to get the high volume of computer-digested information that results. For example, systems used by business executives condense large amounts of information about sales, manufacturing, and transportation into a graphical form that can be quickly interpreted for planning and day-to-day decision-making.

It is useful to think of the human and the computer together as a single cognitive entity, with the computer functioning as a kind of *cognitive co-processor* to the human brain.[*] Low-bandwidth information is transmitted from the human to the computer via the mouse and keyboard, while high-bandwidth information is transmitted back from the computer to the human for flexible pattern discovery via the graphic interface. Each part of the system is doing what it does best. The computer can preprocess vast amounts of information. The human can do rapid pattern analysis and flexible decision-making.

[*]The term "cognitive co-processor" comes from a paper from Stuart Card's famous user interface research lab at Xerox Palo Alto Research Center (PARC) although I am using it in a somewhat different sense here. G. Robertson, S. Card, and J. Mackinlay, 1989. The cognitive co-processor for interactive user interfaces. *Proceedings of the ACM UIST Conference.* 10–18.

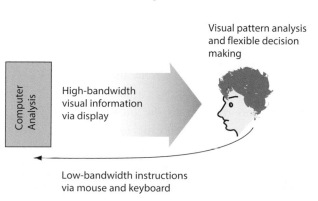

Visual pattern analysis and flexible decision making

Computer Analysis

High-bandwidth visual information via display

Low-bandwidth instructions via mouse and keyboard

Peter Pirolli and Stuart Card developed a theory of information access to help with the design of interfaces to cognitive tools. They began with the *foraging theory* developed by ethologists to account for animal behavior in the wild. Most wild animals spend the bulk of their time in a highly optimized search for food. To survive they must balance the energy expended in finding and consuming food—just eating and digesting has a high cost for grazing animals—with the energy and nutrients obtained. They found that people forage for information on the Internet much as animals forage for food; they are constantly making decisions about what *information scent* (another term from Stuart Card's influential laboratory) to follow, and they try to minimize how much work they must do, offloading tasks onto the computer wherever possible.◆

◆P. Pirolli and S. Card, 1999. Information foraging. *Psychological Review*. 106: 643–675.

The ideal cognitive loop involving a computer is to have it give you exactly the information you need when you need it. This means having only the most relevant information on screen at a given instant. It also means minimizing the cost of getting more information that is related to something already discovered. This is sometimes called *drilling down.*

It might be thought that an eye tracker would provide the ideal method for drilling down, since eye movements are the natural way of getting objects into visual working memory. Eye tracking technology can determine the point of gaze within about one centimeter for an object at arm's length. If the computer could have information about what we are looking at on a display, it might summon up related information without being explicitly asked.

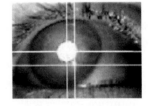

There are two problems with this idea. First, tracking eye movements cheaply and reliably has proven to be technically very difficult. Eye trackers require careful and repeated calibration for each user. Second, when we make eye movements we do not fixate exactly; we usually pick up information in an area of about one centimeter around the fovea at normal computer screen viewing distances and this area can contain several informative objects. This means the computer can only "know" that we might be interested in any of several things. Showing information related to all of them would be more of a hindrance than a help.

The quickest and most practical method for drilling down is the mouse-over *hover query*. Imagine that by moving the mouse over a part of a diagram all the other on-screen information *relating to the thing the mouse is moving over* becomes highlighted and the relevant text enhanced so that it can be easily read. This is exactly what was done by Tamara Munzner and a team at Stanford University in their experimental *Constellation* system.◆ Their application was a kind of network diagram

◆T. Munzner, F. Guimbretiere, and G. Robertson, 1999. Constellation: A visual tool for linguistic queries from MindNet. Proceedings of IEEE *InfoVis*. Conference, San Francisco. 132–135.

showing the relationships between words. The diagram was far too complex to be shown on a screen in any normal way, but by making it interactive hundreds of data objects could be made usable. Compare this to a typical network diagram, in which only between ten and thirty nodes are represented, and the advantage becomes clear. This kind of mouse-over clickless hover query is the next best thing to moving the eyes around an information space. Clickless hover queries can be made only about once a second, slow compared to three-per-second mouse movements, but this still leads to a very rapid interaction where the computer display seems like part of the thinking process, rather than something to be consulted.

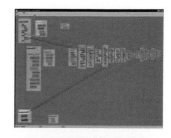

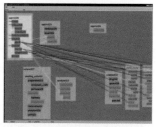

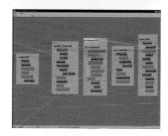

Constellation was a single example of an experimental user interface, but it provides a more general lesson. The ideal computer system that supports visual thinking should be extremely responsive, presenting relevant information just at the moment it is needed. This is not easy to achieve, but something for which to strive.

It should be noted that the most common application of hover queries is in so-called "tooltips." These are the presentation of additional information about a menu item or icon when the mouse is placed over it. Generally these are implemented so that a delay of a second or two occurs between the query and the information display. This is probably appropriate for tooltips because we do not want such information to be constantly popping up, but it would not be appropriate for more tightly coupled human-computer systems. Such a long delay would do serious damage to the efficiency of the cognitive loop that is supported by Constellation.

LEARNING AND THE ECONOMICS OF COGNITION

Many of the visual problems we solve in life seem completely mundane: walking across a room, preparing a salad, looking for a road sign. They are mundane only because we have done them so often that we no longer consider them as requiring thinking at all. When we are born we have little visual skill except the basic minimum needed to identify that something is an "object" and a special propensity to fixate on human faces. Newborns do, however, have the neural architecture which allows the capabilities they can develop.[*] Everything else is a learned skill and these skills make up who we are. Our visual skills vary from the universal, like the ability to reach for and grasp an object, to the very specialized, like determining the sex of chicks, a very difficult visual pattern matching task that can only be done by highly trained experts.

All cognitive activity starts off being difficult and demanding attention. As we develop skills, the neural pathways involved in performing the

[*]One of the most important fixed architectural cognitive capacities is the three-item limit in visual working memory. Even this is somewhat mutable. A recent study showed that video game players can enhance their visual working memory capacities from three to four items. But we do not find people with a working capacity of ten items.

See C.S. Green and D. Bavelier, 2003. Action video game modifies visual selective attention. *Nature*. 423: 534–537.

task are strengthened. These neural pathways carry particular patterns of activation, and strengthening them increases the efficiency of sequences of neural firing (the cognitive activities). The cognitive process becomes more and more automatic and demands less and less high-level attention. The beginning typist must use all his cognitive resources just to find the letters on the keyboard; the expert pays no attention to the keys. The use of drawing tools by an engineer or graphic designer is the same.

Sometimes we have a choice between doing something in an old, familiar way, or in a new way that may be better in the long run. An example is using a new computer-based graphic design package, which is very complex, having hundreds of hard-to-find options. It may take months to become proficient. In such cases we do a kind of cognitive cost-benefit analysis, weighing the considerable cost in time and effort and lost productivity against the benefit of future gains in productivity or quality of work. The professional will always go for tools that give the best results even though they may be the hardest to learn because there is a long-term payoff. For the casual user sophisticated tools are often not worth the effort. This kind of decision-making can be thought of as cognitive economics. Its goal is the optimization of cognitive output.

A designer is often faced with a dilemma that can be considered in terms of cognitive economics. How radical should one make the design? Making radically new designs is more interesting for the designer and leads to kudos from other designers. But radical designs, being novel, take more effort on the part of the consumer. The user must learn the new design conventions and how they can be used. It is usually not worth trying to redesign something that is deeply entrenched, such as the set of international road signs because the cognitive costs, distributed over millions of people, are high. In other areas, innovation can have a huge payoff.

The idea of an economics of cognition can be fruitfully applied at many cognitive scales. In addition to helping us to understand how people make decisions about tool use, it can be used to explain the moment-to-moment prioritization of cognitive operations, and it can even be applied at the level of individual neurons. Sophie Deneve of the *Institute des Sciences Cognitives* in Bron, France, has developed the theory that individual neurons can be considered as *Bayesian* operators, "accumulating evidence about the external world or the body, and communicating to other neurons their certainties about these events." It her persuasive view each neuron is a little machine for turning prior experience into future action.♦

♦In 1763 the Reverend Thomas Bayes came up with a statistical method for optimally combining prior evidence with new evidence in predicting events.

For an application of Bayes' theorem to describe neural activity, see S. Deneve, 2005. Bayesian inference in spiking neurons. Published in *Advances in Neural Information Processing Systems*. Vol. 17. MIT Press 1609–1616.

There are limits, however, to how far we can take the analogy between economic productivity and cognitive productivity. Economics has money as a unifying measure of value. Cognitive processes can be valuable in many different ways and there is potentially no limit on the value of an idea.

DESIGNING FOR MENTAL MODELS

Our brains embody a set of flexibly interconnected mental models of the world and how we operate within it. They are predictive and allow us to take actions knowing the likely consequences. Many of the problems with computer interfaces occur when the user has a mental model of system's operation that does not accurately predict how it behaves. For example, consider the case where a computer appears to be hung up on some task. We do not know if data is taking a long time to arrive, or if the compute program itself has failed. Should we wait or terminate the program? This is a relatively simple problem that can be usually fixed with feedback indicators showing how much data has been loaded. The simple spinning indicators, showing activity, are usually less useful because they can continue to spin even though a program is irretrievably stuck.

Another example where mental models are critical and where visualization is often used is in storm forecasts. Usually weather sites show visualizations of predicted hurricane tracks, wind speeds, and storm surge. However, a study reported in *BAMS* of superstorm Sandy revealed dramatic failures of mental models.[*] People in the affected areas greatly overestimated the danger from high winds, but underestimated the risk from flooding. For one example where action could have been taken, something like 250,000 cars were damaged from flooding and most were subsequently written off, even though in most cases higher ground parking could have been found. In addition, only about 22% of people had an evacuation plan including a place to stay and the traffic conditions associated with late departure were not anticipated.

[*]R.J. Meyer, J. Baker, K. Broad, J. Czajkowski, and B. Orlove, 2014. The dynamics of hurricane risk perception: Real-time evidence from the 2012 Atlantic hurricane season. *Bulletin of the American Meteorological Society*. 95(9): 1389–1404.

Visualizations can be extremely effective means of transmitting executable mental models, as we saw in Chapter 8. But just showing the data—or in this case, the forecasts—is often not enough. Other kinds of visualization such as simple cartoons can help develop the mental models needed for people to realize the true risks.

The problem of providing mental models of computer operations is becoming increasingly important with the new abilities of computer pattern recognition that comes with so-called deep learning. In many cases visualization can help; for example, when computer is used to diagnose cancerous cells, a human radiologist can be shown the most heavily weighed examples of cell that lead to the decision.

WHAT'S NEXT?

The science of human perception is continuing to advance and the account of visual thinking given in this book will, to some extent, be obsolete before it hits the bookstores. As research moves forward, our increasing knowledge of the human brain and perception will lead us in new and exciting directions. I believe, however, that the broad picture of how visual thinking works is essentially correct and will stand the test of time. There is a feeling among vision scientists that the secrets of the brain are at last becoming unlocked and that the outlines of lasting theories are beginning to emerge.

Ultimately the science of perception must take design into account because the designed world is changing people's thinking patterns. Real-world cognition increasingly involves computer-based cognitive tools that are designed to support one mode of thinking or another. This cognitive support environment is developing and evolving from year to year in a process that is happening much faster than evolution. Designed tools can change how people think.

The human brain evolved in a world made up of natural objects: plants, rocks, earth, sky, other humans, and animals. None of these were explicitly designed by early humans, although like other animals, humans have always shaped their environments. Most people now live in cities where almost everything has been designed. Our visual thinking skills are shaped by how we interact with this world of designed objects from the moment we first open our eyes. Objects in our modern environment incorporate computer programs, and some of them are explicitly designed as cognitive tools. At work or at play, many of us are in front of computer screens for a significant percentage of our lives. For many people the manipulation of a mouse or video game controller is as skilled and entrenched as any basic life skill. Many modern teenagers are more skilled at navigating three-dimensional virtual worlds with a game controller than they are at running over rough real-world terrain. Visual design must take into account both the relatively fixed capacities of the human brain as well as the evolving skill sets of people who use sophisticated and powerful cognitive tools. Interactive design is becoming ever more important as the loop coupling humans and computers tightens. The visual system will always be the highest bandwidth sense by far, and making full use of its flexible pattern-finding capabilities can provide great benefits.

Index